DAN-82 DANTES SUBJECT STANDARDIZED TESTS (DSST)

This is your
PASSBOOK for...

Computing and Information Technology

Test Preparation Study Guide
Questions & Answers

NATIONAL LEARNING CORPORATION®

COPYRIGHT NOTICE

This book is SOLELY intended for, is sold ONLY to, and its use is RESTRICTED to individual, bona fide applicants or candidates who qualify by virtue of having seriously filed applications for appropriate license, certificate, professional and/or promotional advancement, higher school matriculation, scholarship, or other legitimate requirements of education and/or governmental authorities.

This book is NOT intended for use, class instruction, tutoring, training, duplication, copying, reprinting, excerption, or adaptation, etc., by:

1) Other publishers
2) Proprietors and/or Instructors of "Coaching" and/or Preparatory Courses
3) Personnel and/or Training Divisions of commercial, industrial, and governmental organizations
4) Schools, colleges, or universities and/or their departments and staffs, including teachers and other personnel
5) Testing Agencies or Bureaus
6) Study groups which seek by the purchase of a single volume to copy and/or duplicate and/or adapt this material for use by the group as a whole without having purchased individual volumes for each of the members of the group
7) Et al.

Such persons would be in violation of appropriate Federal and State statutes.

PROVISION OF LICENSING AGREEMENTS – Recognized educational, commercial, industrial, and governmental institutions and organizations, and others legitimately engaged in educational pursuits, including training, testing, and measurement activities, may address request for a licensing agreement to the copyright owners, who will determine whether, and under what conditions, including fees and charges, the materials in this book may be used them. In other words, a licensing facility exists for the legitimate use of the material in this book on other than an individual basis. However, it is asseverated and affirmed here that the material in this book CANNOT be used without the receipt of the express permission of such a licensing agreement from the Publishers. Inquiries re licensing should be addressed to the company, attention rights and permissions department.

All rights reserved, including the right of reproduction in whole or in part, in any form or by any means, electronic or mechanical, including photocopying, recording, or by any information storage and retrieval system, without permission in writing from the Publisher.

Copyright © 2024 by
National Learning Corporation

212 Michael Drive, Syosset, NY 11791
(516) 921-8888 • www.passbooks.com
E-mail: info@passbooks.com

PUBLISHED IN THE UNITED STATES OF AMERICA

PASSBOOK® SERIES

THE *PASSBOOK® SERIES* has been created to prepare applicants and candidates for the ultimate academic battlefield – the examination room.

At some time in our lives, each and every one of us may be required to take an examination – for validation, matriculation, admission, qualification, registration, certification, or licensure.

Based on the assumption that every applicant or candidate has met the basic formal educational standards, has taken the required number of courses, and read the necessary texts, the *PASSBOOK® SERIES* furnishes the one special preparation which may assure passing with confidence, instead of failing with insecurity. Examination questions – together with answers – are furnished as the basic vehicle for study so that the mysteries of the examination and its compounding difficulties may be eliminated or diminished by a sure method.

This book is meant to help you pass your examination provided that you qualify and are serious in your objective.

The entire field is reviewed through the huge store of content information which is succinctly presented through a provocative and challenging approach – the question-and-answer method.

A climate of success is established by furnishing the correct answers at the end of each test.

You soon learn to recognize types of questions, forms of questions, and patterns of questioning. You may even begin to anticipate expected outcomes.

You perceive that many questions are repeated or adapted so that you can gain acute insights, which may enable you to score many sure points.

You learn how to confront new questions, or types of questions, and to attack them confidently and work out the correct answers.

You note objectives and emphases, and recognize pitfalls and dangers, so that you may make positive educational adjustments.

Moreover, you are kept fully informed in relation to new concepts, methods, practices, and directions in the field.

You discover that you are actually taking the examination all the time: you are preparing for the examination by "taking" an examination, not by reading extraneous and/or supererogatory textbooks.

In short, this PASSBOOK®, used directedly, should be an important factor in helping you to pass your test.

NONTRADITIONAL EDUCATION

Students returning to school as adults bring more varied experience to their studies than do the teenagers who begin college shortly after graduating from high school. As a result, there are numerous programs for students with nontraditional learning curves. Hundreds of colleges and universities grant degrees to people who cannot attend classes at a regular campus or have already learned what the college is supposed to teach.

You can earn nontraditional education credits in many ways:
- Passing standardized exams
- Demonstrating knowledge gained through experience
- Completing campus-based coursework, and
- Taking courses off campus

Some methods of assessing learning for credit are objective, such as standardized tests. Others are more subjective, such as a review of life experiences.

With some help from four hypothetical characters – Alice, Vin, Lynette, and Jorge – this article describes nontraditional ways of earning educational credit. It begins by describing programs in which you can earn a high school diploma without spending 4 years in a classroom. The college picture is more complicated, so it is presented in two parts: one on gaining credit for what you know through course work or experience, and a second on college degree programs. The final section lists resources for locating more information.

Earning High School Credit

People who were prevented from finishing high school as teenagers have several options if they want to do so as adults. Some major cities have back-to-school programs that allow adults to attend high school classes with current students. But the more practical alternatives for most adults are to take the General Educational Development (GED) tests or to earn a high school diploma by demonstrating their skills or taking correspondence classes.

Of course, these options do not match the experience of staying in high school and graduating with one's friends. But they are viable alternatives for adult learners committed to meeting and, often, continuing their educational goals.

GED Program

Alice quit high school her sophomore year and took a job to help support herself, her younger brother, and their newly widowed mother. Now an adult, she wants to earn her high school diploma – and then go on to college. Because her job as head cook and her family responsibilities keep her busy during the day, she plans to get a high school equivalency diploma. She will study for, and take, the GED tests. Every year, about half a million adults earn their high school credentials this way. A GED diploma is accepted in lieu of a high school one by more than 90 percent of employers, colleges, and universities, so it is a good choice for someone like Alice.

The GED testing program is sponsored by the American Council on Education and State and local education departments. It consists of examinations in five subject areas: Writing, science, mathematics, social studies, and literature and the arts. The tests also measure skills such as analytical ability, problem solving, reading comprehension, and ability to understand and apply information. Most of the questions are multiple choice; the writing test includes an essay section on a topic of general interest.

Eligibility rules for taking the exams vary, but some states require that you must be at least 18. Tests are given in English, Spanish, and French. In addition to standard print, versions in large print, Braille, and audiocassette are also available. Total time allotted for the tests is 7 1/2 hours.

The GED tests are not easy. About one-fourth of those who complete the exams every year do not pass. Passing scores are established by administering the tests to a sample of graduating high school seniors. The minimum standard score is set so that about one-third of graduating seniors would not pass the tests if they took them.

Because of the difficulty of the tests, people need to prepare themselves to take them. Often, they start by taking the Official GED Practice Tests, usually available through a local adult education center. Centers are listed in your phone book's blue pages under "Adult Education," "Continuing Education," or "GED." Adult education centers also have information about GED preparation classes and self-study materials. Classes are generally arranged to accommodate adults' work schedules. National Learning Corporation publishes several study guides that aim to thoroughly prepare test-takers for the GED.

School districts, colleges, adult education centers, and community organizations have information about GED testing schedules and practice tests. For more information, contact them, your nearest GED testing center, or:

GED Testing Service
One Dupont Circle, NW, Suite 250
Washington, DC 20036-1163
1(800) 62-MY GED (626-9433)
(202) 939-9490

Skills Demonstration

Adults who have acquired high school level skills through experience might be eligible for the National External Diploma Program. This alternative to the GED does not involve any direct instruction. Instead, adults seeking a high school diploma must demonstrate mastery of 65 competencies in 8 general areas: Communication; computation; occupational preparedness; and self, social, consumer, scientific, and technological awareness.

Mastery is shown through the completion of the tasks. For example, a participant could prove competency in computation by measuring a room for carpeting, figuring out the amount of carpet needed, and computing the cost.

Before being accepted for the program, adults undergo an evaluation. Tests taken at one of the program's offices measure reading, writing, and mathematics abilities. A take-home segment includes a self-assessment of current skills, an individual skill evaluation, and an occupational interest and aptitude test.

Adults accepted for the program have weekly meetings with an assessor. At the meeting, the assessor reviews the participant's work from the previous week. If the task has not been completed properly, the assessor explains the mistake. Participants continue to correct their errors until they master each competency. A high school diploma is awarded upon proven mastery of all 65 competencies.

Fourteen States and the District of Columbia now offer the External Diploma Program. For more information, contact:

External Diploma Program
One Dupont Circle, NW, Suite 250
Washington, DC 20036-1193
(202) 939-9475

Correspondence and Distance Study

Vin dropped out of high school during his junior year because his family's frequent moves made it difficult for him to continue his studies. He promised himself at the time he dropped out that he would someday finish the courses needed for his diploma. For people like Vin, who prefer to earn a traditional diploma in a nontraditional way, there are about a dozen accredited courses of study for earning a high school diploma by correspondence, or distance study. The programs are either privately run, affiliated with a university, or administered by a State education department.

Distance study diploma programs have no residency requirements, allowing students to continue their studies from almost any location. Depending on the course of study, students need not be enrolled full time and usually have more flexible schedules for finishing their work. Selection of courses ranges from vo-tech to college prep, and some programs place different emphasis on the types of diplomas offered. University affiliated schools, for example, allow qualified students to take college courses along with their high school ones. Students can then apply the college credits toward a degree at that university or transfer them to another institution.

Taking courses by distance study is often more challenging and time consuming than attending classes, especially for adults who have other obligations. Success depends on each student's motivation. Students usually do reading assignments on their own. Written exercises, which they complete and send to an instructor for grading, supplement their reading material.

A list of some accredited high schools that offer diplomas by distance study is available free from the Distance Education and Training Council, formerly known as the National Home Study Council. Request the "DETC Directory of Accredited Institutions" from:

The Distance Education and Training Council
1601 18th Street, NW.
Washington, DC 20009-2529
(202) 234-5100

Some publications profiling nontraditional college programs include addresses and descriptions of several high school correspondence ones. See the Resources section at the end of this article for more information.

Getting College Credit For What You Know

Adults can receive college credit for prior coursework, by passing examinations, and documenting experiential learning. With help from a college advisor, nontraditional students should assess their skills, establish their educational goals, and determine the number of college credits they might be eligible for.

Even before you meet with a college advisor, you should collect all your school and training records. Then, make a list of all knowledge and abilities acquired through experience, no matter how irrelevant they seem to your chosen field. Next, determine your educational goals: What specific field do you wish to study? What kind of a degree do you want? Finally, determine how your past work fits into the field of study. Later on, you will evaluate educational programs to find one that's right for you.

People who have complex educational or experiential learning histories might want to have their learning evaluated by the Regents Credit Bank. The Credit Bank, operated by Regents College of the University of the State of New York, allows people to consolidate credits earned through college, experience, or other methods. Special assessments are available for Regents College enrollees whose knowledge in a specific field cannot be adequately evaluated by standardized exams. For more information, contact the Regents Credit Bank at:

Regents College
7 Columbia Circle
Albany, NY 12203-5159
(518) 464-8500

Credit For Prior College Coursework

When Lynette was in college during the 1970s, she attended several different schools and took a variety of courses. She did well in some classes and poorly in others. Now that she is a successful business owner and has more focus, Lynette thinks she should forget about her previous coursework and start from scratch. Instead, she should start from where she is.

Lynette should have all her transcripts sent to the colleges or universities of her choice and let an admissions officer determine which classes are applicable toward a degree. A few credits here and there may not seem like much, but they add up. Even if the subjects do not seem relevant to any major, they might be counted as elective credits toward a degree. And comparing the cost of transcripts with the cost of college courses, it makes sense to spend a few dollars per transcript for a chance to save hundreds, and perhaps thousands, of dollars in books and tuition.

Rules for transferring credits apply to all prior coursework at accredited colleges and universities, whether done on campus or off. Courses completed off campus, often called extended learning, include those available to students through independent study and correspondence. Many schools have extended learning programs; Brigham Young University, for example, offers more than 300 courses through its Department of Independent Study. One type of extended learning is distance learning, a form of correspondence study by technological means such as television, video and audio, CD-ROM, electronic mail, and computer tutorials. See the Resources section at the end of this article for more information about publications available from the National University Continuing Education Association.

Any previously earned college credits should be considered for transfer, no matter what the subject or the grade received. Many schools do not accept the transfer of courses graded below a C or ones taken more than a designated number of years ago. Some colleges and universities also have limits on the number of credits that can be transferred and applied toward a degree. But not all do. For example, Thomas Edison State College, New Jersey's State college for adults, accepts the transfer of all 120 hours of credit required for a baccalaureate degree – provided all the credits are transferred from regionally accredited schools, no more than 80 are at the junior college level, and the student's grades overall and in the field of study average out to C.

To assign credit for prior coursework, most schools require original transcripts. This means you must complete a form or send a written, signed request to have your transcripts released directly to a college or university. Once you have chosen the schools you want to apply to, contact the schools you attended before. Find out how much each transcript costs, and ask them to send your transcripts to the ones you are applying to. Write a letter that includes your name (and names used during attendance, if different) and dates of attendance, along with the names and addresses of the schools to which your transcripts should be sent. Include payment and mail to the registrar at the schools you have attended. The registrar's office will process your request and send an official transcript of your coursework to the colleges or universities you have designated.

Credit For Noncollege Courses

Colleges and universities are not the only ones that offer classes. Volunteer organizations and employers often provide formal training worth college credit. The American Council on Education has two programs that assess thousands of specific courses and make recommendations on the amount of college credit they are worth. Colleges and universities accept the recommendations or use them as guidelines.

One program evaluates educational courses sponsored by government agencies, business and industry, labor unions, and professional and voluntary organizations. It is the Program on Noncollegiate Sponsored Instruction (PONSI). Some of the training seminars Alice has participated in covered topics such as food preparation, kitchen safety, and nutrition. Although she has not yet earned her GED, Alice can earn college credit because of her completion of these formal job-training seminars. The number of credits each seminar is worth does not hinge on Alice's current eligibility for college enrollment.

The other program evaluates courses offered by the Army, Navy, Air Force, Marines, Coast Guard, and Department of Defense. It is the Military Evaluations Program. Jorge has never attended college, but the engineering technology classes he completed as part of his military training are worth college credit. And as an Army veteran, Jorge is eligible for a service that takes the evaluations one step further. The Army/American Council on Education Registry Transcript System (AARTS) will provide Jorge with an individualized transcript of American Council on Education credit recommendations for all courses he completed, the military occupational specialties (MOS's) he held, and examinations he passed while in the Army. All Army and National Guard enlisted personnel and veterans who enlisted after October 1981 are eligible for the transcript. Similar services are being considered by the Navy and Marine Corps.

To obtain a free transcript, see your Army Education Center for a 5454R transcript request form. Include your name, Social Security number, basic active service date, and complete address where you want the transcript sent. Mail your request to:
AARTS Operations Center
415 McPherson Ave.
Fort Leavenworth, KS 66027-1373

Recommendations for PONSI are published in *The National Guide to Educational Credit for Training Programs;* military program recommendations are in *The Guide to the Evaluation of Educational Experiences in the Armed Forces.* See the Resources section at the end of this article for more information about these publications.

Former military personnel who took a foreign language course through the Defense Language Institute may request course transcripts by sending their name, Social Security number, course title, duration of the course, and graduation date to:

Commandant, Defense Language Institute
Attn: ATFL-DAA-AR
Transcripts
Presidio of Monterey
Monterey, CA 93944-5006

Not all of Jorge's and Alice's courses have been assessed by the American Council on Education. Training courses that have no Council credit recommendation should still be assessed by an advisor at the schools they want to attend. Course descriptions, class notes, test scores, and other documentation may be helpful for comparing training courses to their college equivalents. An oral examination or other demonstration of competency might also be required.

There is no guarantee you will receive all the credits you are seeking – but you certainly won't if you make no attempt.

Credit By Examination

Standardized tests are the best-known method of receiving college credit without taking courses. These exams are often taken by high school students seeking advanced placement for college, but they are also available to adult learners. Testing programs and colleges and universities offer exams in a number of subjects. Two U.S. Government institutes have foreign language exams for employees that also may be worth college credit.

It is important to understand that receiving a passing score on these exams does not mean you get college credit automatically. Each school determines which test results it will accept, minimum scores required, how scores are converted for credit, and the amount of credit, if any, to be assigned. Most colleges and universities accept the American Council on Education credit recommendations, published every other year in the 250-page *Guide to Educational Credit by Examination*. For more information, contact:

The American Council on Education
Credit by Examination Program
One Dupont Circle, Suite 250
Washington, DC 20036-1193
(202) 939-9434

Testing programs:

You might know some of the five national testing programs by their acronyms or initials: CLEP, ACT PEP: RCE, DANTES, AP, and NOCTI. (The meanings of these initialisms are explained below.) There is some overlap among programs; for example, four of them have introductory accounting exams. Since you will not be awarded credit more than once for a specific subject, you should carefully evaluate each program for the subject exams you wish to take. And before taking an exam, make sure you will be awarded credit by the college or university you plan to attend.

CLEP (College-Level Examination Program), administered by the College Board, is the most widely accepted of the national testing programs; more than 2,800 accredited schools award credit for passing exam scores. Each test covers material taught in basic

undergraduate courses. There are five general exams – English composition, humanities, college mathematics, natural sciences, and social sciences and history – and many subject exams. Most exams are entirely multiple-choice, but English composition exams may include an essay section. For more information, contact:
>CLEP
>P.O. Box 6600
>Princeton, NJ 08541-6600
>(609) 771-7865

ACT PEP: RCE (American College Testing Proficiency Exam Program: Regents College Examinations) tests are given in 38 subjects within arts and sciences, business, education, and nursing. Each exam is recommended for either lower- or upper-level credit. Exams contain either objective or extended response questions, and are graded according to a standard score, letter grade, or pass/fail. Fees vary, depending on the subject and type of exam. For more information or to request free study guides, contact:
>ACT PEP: Regents College Examinations
>P.O. Box 4014
>Iowa City, IA 52243
>(319) 337-1387
>(New York State residents must contact Regents College directly.)

DANTES (Defense Activity for Nontraditional Education Support) standardized tests are developed by the Educational Testing Service for the Department of Defense. Originally administered only to military personnel, the exams have been available to the public since 1983. About 50 subject tests cover business, mathematics, social science, physical science, humanities, foreign languages, and applied technology. Most of the tests consist entirely of multiple-choice questions. Schools determine their own administering fees and testing schedules. For more information or to request free study sheets, contact:
>DANTES Program Office
>Mail Stop 31-X
>Educational Testing Service
>Princeton, NJ 08541
>1(800) 257-9484

The AP (Advanced Placement) Program is a cooperative effort between secondary schools and colleges and universities. AP exams are developed each year by committees of college and high school faculty appointed by the College Board and assisted by consultants from the Educational Testing Service. Subjects include arts and languages, natural sciences, computer science, social sciences, history, and mathematics. Most tests are 2 or 3 hours long and include both multiple-choice and essay questions. AP courses are available to help students prepare for exams, which are offered in the spring. For more information about the Advanced Placement Program, contact:
>Advanced Placement Services
>P.O. Box 6671
>Princeton, NJ 08541-6671
>(609) 771-7300

NOCTI (National Occupational Competency Testing Institute) assessments are designed for people like Alice, who have vocational-technical skills that cannot be evaluated by other tests. NOCTI assesses competency at two levels: Student/job ready and teacher/experienced worker. Standardized evaluations are available for occupations such as auto-body repair, electronics, mechanical drafting, quantity food preparation, and upholstering. The tests consist of multiple-choice questions and a performance component. Other services include workshops, customized assessments, and pre-testing. For more information, contact:

NOCTI
500 N. Bronson Ave.
Ferris State University
Big Rapids, MI 49307
(616) 796-4699

Colleges and universities:

Many colleges and universities have credit-by-exam programs, through which students earn credit by passing a comprehensive exam for a course offered by the institution. Among the most widely recognized are the programs at Ohio University, the University of North Carolina, Thomas Edison State College, and New York University.

Ohio University offers about 150 examinations for credit. In addition, you may sometimes arrange to take special examinations in non-laboratory courses offered at Ohio University. To take a test for credit, you must enroll in the course. If you plan to transfer the credit earned, you also need written permission from an official at your school. Books and study materials are available, for a cost, through the university. Exams must be taken within 6 months of the enrollment date; most last 3 hours. You may arrange to take the exam off campus if you do not live near the university.

Ohio University is on the quarter-hour system; most courses are worth 4 quarter hours, the equivalent of 3 semester hours. For more information, contact:

Independent Study
Tupper Hall 302
Ohio University
Athens, OH 45701-2979
1(800) 444-2910
(614) 593-2910

The University of North Carolina offers a credit-by-examination option for 140 independent study (correspondence) courses in foreign languages, humanities, social sciences, mathematics, business administration, education, electrical and computer engineering, health administration, and natural sciences. To take an exam, you must request and receive approval from both the course instructor and the independent studies department. Exams must be taken within six months of enrollment, and you may register for no more than two at a time. If you are not near the University's Chapel Hill campus, you may take your exam under supervision at an accredited college, university, community college, or technical institute. For more information, contact:

Independent Studies
CB #1020, The Friday Center
UNC-Chapel Hill
Chapel Hill, NC 27599-1020
1(800) 862-5669 / (919) 962-1134

The Thomas Edison College Examination Program offers more than 50 exams in liberal arts, business, and professional areas. Thomas Edison State College administers tests twice a month in Trenton, New Jersey; however, students may arrange to take their tests with a proctor at any accredited American college or university or U.S. military base. Most of the tests are multiple choice; some also include short answer or essay questions. Time limits range from 90 minutes to 4 hours, depending on the exam. For more information, contact:

Thomas Edison State College
TECEP, Office of Testing and Assessment
101 W. State Street
Trenton, NJ 08608-1176
(609) 633-2844

New York University's Foreign Language Program offers proficiency exams in more than 40 languages, from Albanian to Yiddish. Two exams are available in each language: The 12-point test is equivalent to 4 undergraduate semesters, and the 16-point exam may lead to upper level credit. The tests are given at the university's Foreign Language Department throughout the year.

Proof of foreign language proficiency does not guarantee college credit. Some colleges and universities accept transcripts only for languages commonly taught, such as French and Spanish. Nontraditional programs are more likely than traditional ones to grant credit for proficiency in other languages.

For an informational brochure and registration form for NYU's foreign language proficiency exams, contact:

New York University
Foreign Language Department
48 Cooper Square, Room 107
New York, NY 10003
(212) 998-7030

Government institutes:

The Defense Language Institute and Foreign Service Institute administer foreign language proficiency exams for personnel stationed abroad. Usually, the tests are given at the end of intensive language courses or upon completion of service overseas. But some people – like Jorge, who knows Spanish – speak another language fluently and may be allowed to take a proficiency exam in that language before completing their tour of duty. Contact one of the offices listed below to obtain transcripts of those scores. Proof of proficiency does not guarantee college credit, however, as discussed above.

To request score reports from the Defense Language Institute for Defense Language Proficiency Tests, send your name, Social Security number, language for which you were tested, and, most importantly, when and where you took the exam to:

Commandant, Defense Language Institute
Attn: ATFL-ES-T
DLPT Score Report Request
Presidio of Monterey
Monterey, CA 93944-5006

To request transcripts of scores for Foreign Service Institute exams, send your name, Social Security number, language for which you were tested, and dates or year of exams to:

Foreign Service Institute
Arlington Hall
4020 Arlington Boulevard
Rosslyn, VA 22204-1500
Attn: Testing Office (Send your request to the attention of the testing office of the foreign language in which you were tested)

Credit For Experience

Experiential learning credit may be given for knowledge gained through job responsibilities, personal hobbies, volunteer opportunities, homemaking, and other experiences. Colleges and universities base credit awards on the knowledge you have attained, not for the experience alone. In addition, the knowledge must be college level; not just any learning will do. Throwing horseshoes as a hobby is not likely to be worth college credit. But if you've done research on how and where the sport originated, visited blacksmiths, organized tournaments, and written a column for a trade journal – well, that's a horseshoe of a different color.

Adults attempting to get credit for their experience should be forewarned: Having your experience evaluated for college credit is time-consuming, tedious work – not an easy shortcut for people who want quick-fix college credits. And not all experience, no matter how valuable, is the equivalent of college courses.

Requesting college credit for your experiential learning can be tricky. You should get assistance from a credit evaluations officer at the school you plan to attend, but you should also have a general idea of what your knowledge is worth. A common method for converting knowledge into credit is to use a college catalog. Find course titles and descriptions that match what you have learned through experience, and request the number of credits offered for those courses.

Once you know what credit to ask for, you must usually present your case in writing to officials at the college you plan to attend. The most common form of presenting experiential learning for credit is the portfolio. A portfolio is a written record of your knowledge along with a request for equivalent college credit. It includes an identification and description of the knowledge for which you are requesting credit, an explanatory essay of how the knowledge was gained and how it fits into your educational plans, documentation that you have acquired such knowledge, and a request for college credit. Required elements of a portfolio vary by schools but generally follow those guidelines.

In identifying knowledge you have gained, be specific about exactly what you have learned. For example, it is not enough for Lynette to say she runs a business. She must identify the knowledge she has gained from running it, such as personnel management, tax law, marketing strategy, and inventory review. She must also include brief descriptions about her knowledge of each to support her claims of having those skills.

The essay gives you a chance to relay something about who you are. It should address your educational goals, include relevant autobiographical details, and be well organized, neat, and convey confidence. In his essay, Jorge might first state his goal of becoming an engineer. Then he would explain why he joined the Army, where he got hands-on training and experience in developing and servicing electronic equipment.

This, he would say, led to his hobby of creating remote-controlled model cars, of which he has built 20. His conclusion would highlight his accomplishments and tie them to his desire to become an electronic engineer.

Documentation is evidence that you've learned what you claim to have learned. You can show proof of knowledge in a variety of ways, including audio or video recordings, letters from current or former employers describing your specific duties and job performance, blueprints, photographs or artwork, and transcripts of certifying exams for professional licenses and certification – such as Alice's certification from the American Culinary Federation. Although documentation can take many forms, written proof alone is not always enough. If it is impossible to document your knowledge in writing, find out if your experiential learning can be assessed through supplemental oral exams by a faculty expert.

Earning a College Degree

Nontraditional students often have work, family, and financial obligations that prevent them from quitting their jobs to attend school full time. Can they still meet their educational goals? Yes.

More than 150 accredited colleges and universities have nontraditional bachelor's degree programs that require students to spend little or no time on campus; over 300 others have nontraditional campus-based degree programs. Some of those schools, as well as most junior and community colleges, offer associate's degrees nontraditionally. Each school with a nontraditional course of study determines its own rules for awarding credit for prior coursework, exams, or experience, as discussed previously. Most have charges on top of tuition for providing these special services.

Several publications profile nontraditional degree programs; see the Resources section at the end of this article for more information. To determine which school best fits your academic profile and educational goals, first list your criteria. Then, evaluate nontraditional programs based on their accreditation, features, residency requirements, and expenses. Once you have chosen several schools to explore further, write to them for more information. Detailed explanations of school policies should help you decide which ones you want to apply to.

Get beyond the printed word – especially the glowing words each school writes about itself. Check out the schools you are considering with higher education authorities, alumni, employers, family members, and friends. If possible, visit the campus to talk to students and instructors and sit in on a few classes, even if you will be completing most or all of your work off campus. Ask school officials questions about such things as enrollment numbers, graduation rate, faculty qualifications, and confusing details about the application process or academic policies. After you have thoroughly investigated each prospective college or university, you can make an informed decision about which is right for you.

Accreditation

Accreditation is a process colleges and universities submit to voluntarily for getting their credentials. An accredited school has been investigated and visited by teams of observers and has periodic inspections by a private accrediting agency. The initial review can take two years or more.

Regional agencies accredit entire schools, and professional agencies accredit either specialized schools or departments within schools. Although there are no national accrediting standards, not just any accreditation will do. Countless "accreditation associations" have been invented by schools, many of which have no academic programs and sell phony degrees, to accredit themselves. But 6 regional and about 80 professional accrediting associations in the United States are recognized by the U.S. Department of Education or the Commission on Recognition of Postsecondary Accreditation. When checking accreditation, these are the names to look for. For more information about accreditation and accrediting agencies, contact:

> Institutional Participation Oversight Service Accreditation and State Liaison Division
> U.S. Department of Education
> ROB 3, Room 3915
> 600 Independence Ave., SW
> Washington, DC 20202-5244
> (202) 708-7417

Because accreditation is not mandatory, lack of accreditation does not necessarily mean a school or program is bad. Some schools choose not to apply for accreditation, are in the process of applying, or have educational methods too unconventional for an accrediting association's standards. For the nontraditional student, however, earning a degree from a college or university with recognized accreditation is an especially important consideration. Although nontraditional education is becoming more widely accepted, it is not yet mainstream. Employers skeptical of a degree earned in a nontraditional manner are likely to be even less accepting of one from an unaccredited school.

Program Features

Because nontraditional students have diverse educational objectives, nontraditional schools are diverse in what they offer. Some programs are geared toward helping students organize their scattered educational credits to get a degree as quickly as possible. Others cater to those who may have specific credits or experience but need assistance in completing requirements. Whatever your educational profile, you should look for a program that works with you in obtaining your educational goals.

A few nontraditional programs have special admissions policies for adult learners like Alice, who plan to earn their GEDs but want to enroll in college in the meantime. Other features of nontraditional programs include individualized learning agreements, intensive academic counseling, cooperative learning and internship placement, and waiver of some prerequisites or other requirements – as well as college credit for prior coursework, examinations, and experiential learning, all discussed previously.

Lynette, whose primary goal is to finish her degree, wants to earn maximum credits for her business experience. She will look for programs that do not limit the number of credits awarded for equivalency exams and experiential learning. And since well-documented proof of knowledge is essential for earning experiential learning credits, Lynette should make sure the program she chooses provides assistance to students submitting a portfolio.

Jorge, on the other hand, has more credits than he needs in certain areas and is willing to forego some. To become an engineer, he must have a bachelor's degree; but because he is accustomed to hands-on learning, Jorge is interested in getting experience as he gains more technical skills. He will concentrate on finding schools with strong cooperative education, supervised fieldwork, or internship programs.

Residency Requirements

Programs are sometimes deemed nontraditional because of their residency requirements. Many people think of residency for colleges and universities in terms of tuition, with in-state students paying less than out-of-state ones. Residency also may refer to where a student lives, either on or off campus, while attending school.

But in nontraditional education, residency usually refers to how much time students must spend on campus, regardless of whether they attend classes there. In some nontraditional programs, students need not ever step foot on campus. Others require only a very short residency, such as one day or a few weeks. Many schools have standard residency requirements of several semesters but schedule classes for evenings or weekends to accommodate working adults.

Lynette, who previously took courses by independent study, prefers to earn credits by distance study. She will focus on schools that have no residency requirement. Several colleges and universities have nonresident degree completion programs for adults with some college credit. Under the direction of a faculty advisor, students devise a plan for earning their remaining credits. Methods for earning credits include independent study, distance learning, seminars, supervised fieldwork, and group study at arranged sites. Students may have to earn a certain number of credits through the degree-granting institution. But many programs allow students to take courses at accredited schools of their choice for transfer toward their degree.

Alice wants to attend lectures but has an unpredictable schedule. Her best course of action will be to seek out short residency programs that require students to attend seminars once or twice a semester. She can take courses that are televised and videotape them to watch when her schedule permits, with the seminars helping to ensure that she properly completes her coursework. Many colleges and universities with short residency requirements also permit students to earn some credits elsewhere, by whatever means the student chooses.

Some fields of study require classroom instruction. As Jorge will discover, few colleges and universities allow students to earn a bachelor's degree in engineering entirely through independent study. Nontraditional residency programs are designed to accommodate adults' daytime work schedules. Jorge should look for programs offering evening, weekend, summer, and accelerated courses.

Tuition and Other Expenses

The final decisions about which schools Alice, Jorge, and Lynette attend may hinge in large part on a single issue: Cost. And rising tuition is only part of the equation. Beginning with application fees and continuing through graduation fees, college expenses add up.

Traditional and nontraditional students have some expenses in common, such as the cost of books and other materials. Tuition might even be the same for some courses, especially for colleges and universities offering standard ones at unusual times. But for nontraditional programs, students may also pay fees for services such as credit or transcript review, evaluation, advisement, and portfolio assessment.

Students are also responsible for postage and handling or setup expenses for independent study courses, as well as for all examination and transcript fees for transferring credits. Usually, the more nontraditional the program, the more detailed the fees. Some schools charge a yearly enrollment fee rather than tuition for degree completion candidates who want their files to remain active.

Although tuition and fees might seem expensive, most educators tell you not to let money come between you and your educational goals. Talk to someone in the financial aid department of the school you plan to attend or check your library for publications about financial aid sources. The U.S. Department of Education publishes a guide to Federal aid programs such as Pell Grants, student loans, and work-study. To order the free 74-page booklet, *The Student Guide: Financial Aid from the U.S. Department of Education,* contact:

    Federal Student Aid Information Center
    P.O. Box 84
    Washington, DC 20044
    1 (800) 4FED-AID (433-3243)

Resources

Information on how to earn a high school diploma or college degree without following the usual routes is available from several organizations and in numerous publications. Information on nontraditional graduate degree programs, available for master's through doctoral level, though not discussed in this article, can usually be obtained from the same resources that detail bachelor's degree programs.

National Learning Corporation publishes study guides for all of these exams, for both general examinations and tests in specific subject areas. To order study guides, or to browse their catalog featuring more than 5,000 titles, visit NLC online at www.passbooks.com, or contact them by phone at (800) 632-8888.

Organizations

Adult learners should always contact their local school system, community college, or university to learn about programs that are readily available. The following national organizations can also supply information:

    American Council on Education
    One Dupont Circle
    Washington, DC 20036-1193
    (202) 939-9300

Within the American Council on Education, the Center for Adult Learning and Educational Credentials administers the National External Diploma Program, the GED Program, the Program on Noncollegiate Sponsored Instruction, the Credit by Examination Program, and the Military Evaluations Program.

DANTES Subject Standardized Tests

INTRODUCTION

The DANTES (Defense Activity for Non-Traditional Education Support) subject standardized tests are comprehensive college and graduate level examinations given by the Armed Forces, colleges and graduate schools as end-of-subject course evaluation final examinations or to obtain college equivalency credits in the various subject areas tested.

The DANTES Examination Program enables students to obtain college credit for what they have learned on the job, through self-study, personal interest, correspondence courses or by any other means. It is used by colleges and universities to award college credit to students who demonstrate that they know as much as students completing an equivalent college course. It is a cost-efficient, time-saving way for students to use their knowledge to accomplish their educational goals.

Most schools accept the American Council on Education (ACE) recommendations for the minimum score required and the amount of credit awarded, but not all schools do. Be sure to check the policy regarding the score level required for credit and the number of credits to be awarded.

Not all tests are accepted by all institutions. Even when a test is accepted by an institution, it may not be acceptable for every program at that institution. Before considering testing, ascertain the acceptability of a specific test for a particular course.

Colleges and universities that administer DANTES tests may administer them to any applicant – or they may administer the tests only to students registered at their institution. Decisions about who will be allowed to test are made by the school. Students should contact the test center to determine current policies and schedules for DANTES testing.

Colleges and universities authorized to administer DANTES tests usually do so throughout the calendar year. Each school sets its own fee for test administration and establishes its own testing schedule. Contact the representative at the administering school directly to make arrangements for testing.

Checklist
For Students

- ✓ Visit **www.getcollegecredit.com** to obtain a list of tests, fact sheets, test preparation materials, participating colleges and universities, and much more.

- ✓ Contact your school advisor to confirm that the DSST you selected will fit into your curriculum.

- ✓ Consult the ***DSST Candidate Information Bulletin*** for answers to specific questions.

- ✓ Contact the test site to schedule your test.

- ✓ Prepare for your examination by using the fact sheet as a guide.

- ✓ Take the test.

If you would like a score report sent to your college or university, it is a good idea to bring the four-digit code with you. You must write the DSST Test Center Code for that institution on your answer sheet at the time of testing. DSST Test Center Codes are noted in the DSST Participating Colleges and Universities listing on the Web site.

If you prefer to send a score report to an institution at a later date, there is a transcript fee of $20 for each transcript ordered.

Thomson Prometric
DSST Program
2000 Lenox Drive, Third Floor
Lawrenceville, NJ 08648

Toll-free: 877-471-9860
609-895-5011

E-mail: pnj-dsst@thomson.com

MAKING A COLLEGE DEGREE WITHIN YOUR REACH

Today, there are many educational alternatives to the classroom—you can learn from your job, your reading, your independent study, and special interests you pursue. You may already have learned the subject matter covered by some college-level courses.

The DSST Program is a nationally recognized testing program that gives you the opportunity to receive college credit for learning acquired outside the traditional college classroom. Colleges and universities throughout the United States administer the program, developed by Thomson Prometric, year-round. Annually, over 90,000 DSSTs are administered to individuals who are interested in continuing their education. Take advantage of the DSST testing program; it speeds the educational process and provides the flexibility adults need, making earning a degree more feasible.

Since requirements differ from college to college, please check with the credit-awarding institution before taking a DSST. More than 1,800 colleges and universities currently award credit for DSSTs, and the number is growing every day. You can choose from 37 test titles in the areas of Social Science, Business, Mathematics, Applied Technology, Humanities, and Physical Science. A brief description of each examination is found on the pages that follow.

Reach Your Career Goals Through DSSTs

Use DSSTs to help you earn your degree, get a promotion, or simply demonstrate that you have college-level knowledge in subjects relevant to your work.

Save Time...

You don't have to sit through classes when you have previously acquired the knowledge or experience for most of what is being taught and can learn the rest yourself. You might be able to bypass introductory-level courses in subject areas you already know.

Save Money...

DSSTs save you money because the classes you bypass by earning credit through the DSST Program are classes you won't have to pay for on your way to earning your degree. You can use the money instead to take more advanced courses that can be more challenging and rewarding.

Improve Your Chances for Admission to College

Each college has its own admission policies; however, having passing scores for DSSTs on your transcript can provide strong evidence of how well you can perform at the college level.

Gain Confidence Performing at a College Level

Many adults returning to college find that lack of confidence is often the greatest hurdle to overcome. Passing a DSST demonstrates your ability to perform on a college level.

Make Up for Courses You May Have Missed

You may be ready to graduate from college and find that you are a few credits short of earning your degree. By using semester breaks, vacation time, or leisure time to study independently, you can prepare to take one or more DSSTs, fulfill your academic requirements, and graduate on time.

If You Cannot Attend Regularly Scheduled Classes...

If your lifestyle or responsibilities prevent you from attending regularly scheduled classes, you can earn your college degree from a college offering an external degree program. The DSST Program allows you to earn your degree by study and experience outside the traditional classroom.

Many colleges and universities offer external degree or distance learning programs. For additional information, contact the college you plan to attend or:

Center for Lifelong Learning
American Council on Education
One DuPont Circle NW, Suite 250
Washington, DC 20036
202-939-9475
www.acenet.edu
(Select "Center for Lifelong Learning" under "Programs & Services"
for more information)

Fact Sheets

For each test, there is a Fact Sheet that outlines the topics covered by each test and includes a list of sample questions, a list of recommended references of books that would be useful for review, and the number of credits awarded for a passing score as recommended by the American Council on Education (ACE). *Please note that some schools require scores that are higher than the minimum ACE-recommended passing score.* It is suggested that you check with your college or university to determine what score they require in order to earn credit. You can obtain Fact Sheets by:
- Downloading them from www.getcollegecredit.com
- E-mailing a request to pnj-dsst@thomson.com
- Completing a Candidate Publications Order Form

DSST Online Practice Tests

DSST online practice tests contain items that reflect a *partial range of difficulty* identified in the Content Outline section on each Fact Sheet. There is an online DSST Practice Test in the following categories:
- Mathematics
- Social Science
- Business
- Physical Science
- Applied Technology
- Humanities

Although the online DSST Practice Test questions do not indicate the full range of difficulty you would find in an actual DSST test, they will help you assess your knowledge level. Each online DSST Practice Test can be purchased by visiting www.getcollegecredit.com and clicking on DSST Practice Exams.

TAKING DSST EXAMINATIONS

Earning College Credit for DSST Examinations
To find out if the college of your choice awards credit for passing DSST scores, contact the admissions office or counseling and testing office. The college can also provide information on the scores required for awarding credit, the number of credit hours awarded, and any courses that can be bypassed with satisfactory scores.

It is important that you contact the institution of your choice as early as possible since credit-awarding policies differ among colleges and universities.

Where to Take DSSTs
DSSTs are administered at colleges and universities nationwide. Each location determines the frequency and scheduling of test administrations. To obtain the most current list of participating DSST colleges and universities:
- Visit and download the information from www.getcollegecredit.com
- E-mail pnj-dsst@thomson.com

Scheduling Your Examination
Please be aware that some colleges and universities provide DSST testing services to enrolled students only. After you have selected a college or university that administers DSSTs, you will need to contact them to schedule your test date.

The fee to take a DSST is $60 per test. This fee entitles you to two score reports after the test is scored. One will be sent directly to you and the other will be sent to the college or university that you designate on your answer sheet. You may pay the test fee with a certified check or U.S. money order made payable to Thomson Prometric or you may charge the test fee to your Visa, MasterCard or American Express credit card. Note: The credit card statement will reflect a charge from Thomson Prometric for all DSST examinations. *(Declined credit card charges will be assessed an additional $25 processing fee.)*

In addition, the test site may also require a test administration fee for each examination, to be paid directly to the institution. Contact the test site to determine its administration fee and payment policy.

Other Testing Arrangements
If you are unable to find a participating DSST college or university in your area, you may want to contact the testing office of a local accredited college or university to determine whether a representative from that office will agree to administer the test(s) for you.

The school's representative should then contact the DSST Program at 866-794-3497 to arrange for this administration. If you are unable to locate a test site, contact Thomson Prometric for assistance at pnj-dsst@thomson.com or 866-794-3497.

Testing Accommodations for Students with Disabilities
Thomson Prometric is committed to serving test takers with disabilities by providing services and reasonable testing accommodations as set forth in the provisions of the *Americans with Disabilities Act* (ADA). If you have a disability, as prescribed by the ADA, and require special testing services or arrangements, please contact the test administrator at the test site. You will be asked to submit to the test administrator documentation of your disability and your request for special accommodations. The test

administrator will then forward your documentation along with your request for testing accommodations to Thomson Prometric for approval.

Please submit your request as far in advance of your test date as possible so that the necessary accommodations can be made. Only test takers with documented disabilities are eligible for special accommodations.

On the Day of the Examination

It is important to review this information and to have the correct identification present on the day of the examination:

- Arrive on time as a courtesy to the test administrator.
- Bring a valid form of government-issued identification that includes a current photo and your signature (acceptable documents include a driver's license, passport, state-issued identification card or military identification). *Anyone who fails to present valid identification will not be allowed to test.*
- Bring several No. 2 (soft-lead) sharpened pencils with good erasers, a watch, and a black pen if you will be writing an essay.
- Do not bring books or papers.
- Do not bring an alarm watch that beeps, a telephone, or a phone beeper into the testing room.
- The use of nonprogrammable calculators, slide rules, scratch paper and/or other materials is permitted for some of the tests.

DSST SCORING POLICIES

Your DSST examination scores are reported only to you, unless you request that they be sent elsewhere. If you want your scores sent to your college, you must provide the correct DSST code number of the school on your answer sheet at the time you take the test. See the *DSST Directory of Colleges and Universities* on the Web site www.getcollegecredit.com.

If your institution is not listed, contact Thomson Prometric at 866-794-3497 to establish a code number. (Some schools may require a student to be enrolled prior to receiving a score report.)

Receiving Your Score Report

Allow approximately four weeks after testing to receive your score report.

Calling DSST Customer Service before the required four-week score processing time has elapsed will not expedite the processing of your scores. Due to privacy and security requirements, scores will not be reported to students over the telephone under any circumstance.

Scoring of Principles of Public Speaking Speeches

The speech portion of the *Principles of Public Speaking* examination will be sent to speech raters who are faculty members at accredited colleges that currently teach or have previously taught the course. Scores for the *Principles of Public Speaking* examination are available six to eight weeks from receipt by Thomson Prometric. If you take the *Principles of Public Speaking* examination and fail (either the objective, speech portion, or both), you must follow the retesting policy waiting period of six months (180 days) before retaking the entire exam.

Essays

The essays for *Ethics in America* and *Technical Writing* are <u>optional</u> and thus are not scored by raters. The essays are forwarded to the college or university that you designate, along with your score report, for their use in determining the award of credit. <u>Before taking the *Ethics in America* or *Technical Writing* examinations, check with your college or university to determine whether the essay is required.</u>

NOTE: *Principles of Public Speaking* speech topic cassette tapes and essays are kept on file at Thomson Prometric for one year from the date of administration.

How to Get Transcripts

There is a $20 fee for each transcript you request. Payment must be in the form of a certified check, U.S. money order payable to Thomson Prometric, or credit card. Personal checks and debit cards are NOT an acceptable method of payment. One transcript may include scores for one or more examinations taken. To request a transcript, download the Transcript Order Form from www.getcollegecredit.com.

DESCRIPTION OF THE DSST EXAMINATIONS

Mathematics

- **Fundamentals of College Algebra** covers mathematical concepts such as fundamental algebraic operations; linear, absolute value; quadratic equations, inequalities, radials, exponents and logarithms, factoring polynomials and graphing. The use of a nonprogrammable, handheld calculator is permitted.

- **Principles of Statistics** tests the understanding of the various topics of statistics, both qualitatively and quantitatively, and the ability to apply statistical methods to solve a variety of problems. The topics included in this test are descriptive statistics; correlation and regression; probability; chance models and sampling and tests of significance. The use of a nonprogrammable, handheld calculator is permitted.

Social Science

- **Art of the Western World** deals with the history of art during the following periods: classical; Romanesque and Gothic; early Renaissance; high Renaissance, Baroque; rococo; neoclassicism and romanticism; realism, impressionism and post-impressionism; early twentieth century; and post-World War II.

- **Western Europe Since 1945** tests the knowledge of basic facts and terms and the understanding of concepts and principles related to the areas of the historical background of the aftermath of the Second World War and rebuilding of Europe; national political systems; issues and policies in Western European societies; European institutions and processes; and Europe's relations with the rest of the world.

- **An Introduction to the Modern Middle East** emphasizes core knowledge (including geography, Judaism, Christianity, Islam, ethnicity); nineteenth-century European impact; twentieth-century Western influences; World Wars I and II; new nations; social and cultural changes (1900-1960) and the Middle East from 1960 to present.

- **Human/Cultural Geography** includes the Earth and basic facts (coordinate systems, maps, physiography, atmosphere, soils and vegetation, water); culture and environment, spatial processes (social processes, modern economic systems, settlement patterns, political geography); and regional geography.

- **Rise and Fall of the Soviet Union** covers Russia under the Old Regime; the Revolutionary Period; New Economic Policy; Pre-war Stalinism; The Second World War; Post-war Stalinism; The Khrushchev Years; The Brezhnev Era; and reform and collapse.

- **A History of the Vietnam War** covers the history of the roots of the Vietnam War; the First Vietnam War (1946-1954); pre-war developments (1954-1963); American involvement in the Vietnam War; Tet (1968); Vietnamizing the War (1968-1973); Cambodia and Laos; peace; legacies and lessons.

- **The Civil War and Reconstruction** covers the Civil War from presecession (1861) through Reconstruction. It includes causes of the war; secession; Fort Sumter; the war in the east and in the west; major battles; the political situation; assassination of Lincoln; end of the Confederacy; and Reconstruction.

- **Foundations of Education** includes topics such as contemporary issues in education; past and current influences on education (philosophies, democratic ideals, social/economic influences); and the interrelationships between contemporary issues and influences.

- **Life-span Developmental Psychology** covers models and theories; methods of study; ethical issues; biological development; perception, learning and memory; cognition and language; social, emotional, and personality development; social behaviors, family life cycle, extrafamilial settings; singlehood and cohabitation; occupational development and retirement; adjustment to life stresses; and bereavement and loss.

- **Drug and Alcohol Abuse** includes such topics as drug use in society; classification of drugs; pharmacological principles; alcohol (types, effects of, alcoholism); general principles and use of sedative hypnotics, narcotic analgesics, stimulants, and hallucinogens; other drugs (inhalants, steroids); and prevention/treatment.

- **General Anthropology** deals with anthropology as a discipline; theoretical perspectives; physical anthropology; archaeology; social organization; economic organization; political organization; religion; and modernization and application of anthropology.

- **Introduction to Law Enforcement** includes topics such as history and professional movement of law enforcement; overview of the U.S. criminal justice system; police systems in the U.S.; police organization, management, and issues; and U.S. law and precedents.

- **Criminal Justice** deals with criminal behavior (crime in the U.S., theories of crime, types of crime); the criminal justice system (historical origins, legal foundations, due process); police; the court system (history and organization, adult court system, juvenile court, pre-trial and post-trial processes); and corrections.

- **Fundamentals of Counseling** covers historical development (significant influences and people); counselor roles and functions; the counseling relationship; and theoretical approaches to counseling.

Business
- **Principles of Finance** deals with financial statements and planning; time value of money; working capital management; valuation and characteristics; capital budgeting; cost of capital; risk and return; and international financial management. The use of a nonprogrammable, handheld calculator is permitted.

- **Principles of Financial Accounting** includes topics such as general concepts and principles, accounting cycle and classification; transaction analysis; accruals and deferrals; cash and internal control; current accounts; long- and short-term liabilities; capital stock; and financial statements. The use of a nonprogrammable, handheld calculator is permitted.

- **Human Resource Management** covers general employment issues; job analysis; training and development; performance appraisals; compensation issues; security issues; personnel legislation and regulation; labor relations and current issues; an overview of the Human Resource Management Field; Human Resource Planning; Staffing; training and development; compensation issues; safety and health; employee rights and discipline; employment law; labor relations and current issues and trends.

- **Organizational Behavior** deals with the study of organizational behavior (scientific approaches, research designs, data collection methods); individual processes and characteristics; interpersonal and group processes and characteristics; organizational processes and characteristics; and change and development processes.

- **Principles of Supervision** deals with the roles and responsibilities of the supervisor; management functions (planning, organization and staffing, directing at the supervisory level); and other topics (legal issues, stress management, union environments, quality concerns).

- **Business Law II** covers topics such as sales of goods; debtor and creditor relations; business organizations; property; and commercial paper.

- **Introduction to Computing** includes topics such as history and technological generations; hardware/software; applications to information technology; program development; data management; communications and connectivity; and computing and society. The use of a nonprogrammable, handheld calculator is permitted.

- **Management Information Systems** covers systems theory, analysis and design of systems, hardware and software; database management; telecommunications; management of the MIS functional area and informational support.

- **Introduction to Business** deals with economic issues affecting business; international business; government and business; forms of business ownership; small business, entrepreneurship and franchise; management process; human resource management; production and operations; marketing management; financial management; risk management and insurance; and management and information systems.

- **Money and Banking** covers the role and kinds of money; commercial banks and other financial intermediaries; central banking and the Federal Reserve system; money and macroeconomics activity; monetary policy in the U.S.; and the international monetary system.

- **Personal Finance** includes topics such as financial goals and values; budgeting; credit and debt; major purchases; taxes; insurance; investments; and retirement and estate planning. The use of auxiliary materials, such as calculators and slide rules, is NOT permitted.

- **Business Mathematics** deals with basic operations with integers, fractions, and decimals; round numbers; ratios; averages; business graphs; simple interest; compound interest and annuities; net pay and deductions; discounts and markups; depreciation and net worth; corporate securities; distribution of ownership; and stock and asset turnover.

Physical Science
• **Astronomy** covers the history of astronomy, celestial mechanics; celestial systems; astronomical instruments; the solar system; nature and evolution; the galaxy; the universe; determining astronomical distances; and life in the universe.

• **Here's to Your Health** covers mental health and behavior; human development and relationships; substance abuse; fitness and nutrition; risk factors, disease, and disease prevention; and safety, consumer awareness, and environmental concerns.

• **Environment and Humanity** deals with topics such as ecological concepts (ecosystems, global ecology, food chains and webs); environmental impacts; environmental management and conservation; and political processes and the future.

• **Principles of Physical Science I** includes physics: Newton's Laws of Motion; energy and momentum; thermodynamics; wave and optics; electricity and magnetism; chemistry: properties of matter; atomic theory and structure; and chemical reactions.

• **Physical Geology** covers Earth materials; igneous, sedimentary, and metamorphic rocks; surface processes (weathering, groundwater, glaciers, oceanic systems, deserts and winds, hydrologic cycle); internal Earth processes; and applications (mineral and energy resources, environmental geology).

Applied Technology
• **Technical Writing** covers topics such as theory and practice of technical writing; purpose, content, and organizational patterns of common types of technical documents; elements of various technical reports; and technical editing. Students have the option to write a short essay on one of the technical topics provided. Thomson Prometric will not score the essay; however, for determining the award of credit, a copy of the essay will be forwarded to the college or university you've designated along with the score report or transcript.

Humanities
• **Ethics in America** deals with ethical traditions (Greek views, Biblical traditions, moral law, consequential ethics, feminist ethics); ethical analysis of issues arising in interpersonal and personal-societal relationships and in professional and occupational roles; and relationships between ethical traditions and the ethical analysis of situations. Students have the option to write an essay to analyze a morally problematic situation in terms of issues relevant to a decision and arguments for alternative positions. Thomson Prometric will not score the essay; however, for determining the award of credit, a copy of the essay will be forwarded to the college or university you've designated along with the score report or transcript.

• **Introduction to World Religions** covers topics such as dimensions and approaches to religion; primal religions; Hinduism; Buddhism; Confucianism; Taoism; Judaism; Christianity; and Islam.

• **Principles of Public Speaking** consists of two parts: Part One consists of multiple-choice questions covering considerations of Principles of Public Speaking; audience analysis; purposes of speeches; structure/organization; content/supporting materials; research; language and style; delivery; communication apprehension; listening and feedback; and criticism and evaluation. Part Two requires the student to record an impromptu persuasive speech that will be scored.

FREQUENTLY ASKED QUESTIONS ABOUT DSSTs

In order to pass the test, must I study from one of the recommended references?
The recommended references are a listing of books that were being used as textbooks in college courses of the same or similar title at the time the test was developed. Appropriate textbooks for study are not limited to those listed in the fact sheet. If you wish to obtain study resources to prepare for the examination, you may reference either the current edition of the listed titles or textbooks currently used at a local college or university for the same class title. It is recommended that you reference more than one textbook on the topics outlined in the fact sheet. You should begin by checking textbook content against the content outline included on the front page of the DSST fact sheet before selecting textbooks that cover the text content from which to study. Textbooks may be found at the campus bookstore of a local college or university offering a course on the subject.

Is there a penalty for guessing on the tests?
There is no penalty for guessing on DSSTs, so you should mark an answer for each question.

How much time will I have to complete the test?
Many DSSTs can be completed within 90 minutes; however, additional time can be allowed if necessary.

What should I do if I find a test question irregularity?
Continue testing and then report the irregularity to the test administrator after the test. This may be done by asking that the test administrator note the irregularity on the Supervisor's Irregularity Report or you can write to Thomson Prometric, DSST Program, 2000 Lenox Drive, Third Floor, Lawrenceville, NJ 08648, and indicate the form and question number(s) or circumstances as well as your name and address.

When will I receive my score report?
Allow approximately four weeks from the date of testing to receive your score report. Allow six to eight weeks to receive a score report for the *Principles of Public Speaking* examination.

Will my test scores be released without my permission?
Your test score will not be released to anyone other than the school you designate on your answer sheet unless you write to us and ask us to send a transcript elsewhere. Instructions about how to do this can be found on your score report. Your scores may be used for research purposes, but individual scores are never made public nor are individuals identified if research findings are made public.

If I do not achieve a passing score on the test, how long must I wait until I can take the test again?
If you do not receive a score on the test that will enable you to obtain credit for the course, you may take the test again after six months (180 days). Please do not attempt to take the test before six months (180 days) have passed because you will receive a score report marked *invalid* and your test fee will not be refunded.

Can my test scores be canceled?

The test administrator is required to report any irregularities to Thomson Prometric. <u>The consequence of bringing unauthorized materials into the testing room, or giving or receiving help, will be the forfeiture of your test fee and the invalidation of test scores.</u> The DSST Program reserves the right to cancel scores and not issue score reports in such situations.

What can I do if I feel that my test scores were not accurately reported?

Thomson Prometric recognizes the extreme importance of test results to candidates and has a multi-step quality-control procedure to help ensure that reported scores are accurate. If you have reason to believe that your score(s) were not accurately reported, you may request to have your answer sheet reviewed and hand scored.

The fees for this service are:
- $20 fee if requested within six months of the test date
- $30 fee if requested more than six months from the test date
- $30 fee if a re-evaluation of the *Principles of Public Speaking* speech is requested

The fee for this service can be paid by credit card or by certified check or U.S. money order payable to Thomson Prometric. Submit your request for score verification along with the appropriate fee or credit card information (credit card number and expiration date) to Thomson Prometric, DSST Program, 2000 Lenox Drive, Third Floor, Lawrenceville, NJ 08648. Include your full name, the test title, the date you took the test, and your Social Security number. Candidates will be notified if a scoring discrepancy is discovered within four weeks of receipt of the request.

What does ACE recommendation mean?

The ACE recommendation is the minimum passing score recommended by the American Council on Education for any given test. It is equivalent to the average score of students in the DSST norming sample who received a grade of C for the course. Some schools require a score higher than the ACE recommendation.

Who is NLC?

National Learning Corporation (NLC) has been successfully preparing candidates for 40 years for over 5,000 exams. NLC publishes Passbook® study guides to help candidates prepare for all DANTES and CLEP exams and almost every other type of exam from high school through adult career.

Go to our website — www.passbooks.com — or call (800) 632-8888 for information about ordering our Passbooks.

To get detailed information on the DSST program and DSST preparation materials, visit www.getcollegecredit.com.

If you are interested in taking the DSST exams, call 877-471-9860 or e-mail pnj-dsst@thomson.com.

COMPUTING AND INFORMATION TECHNOLOGY
(Formerly, Introduction to Computing

EXAM INFORMATION

This exam was developed to enable schools to award credit to students for knowledge equivalent to that learned by students taking the course. This exam tests the ability to understand hardware, software licensing and development tools; development life cycles; data management; connectivity, privacy concerns; intellectual property; network etiquette; telecommunications law; artificial intelligence, and globalization.

The exam contains 100 questions to be answered in 2 hours.

The use of nonprogrammable calculators is permitted during the test. Scratch paper for computations will be provided. A calculator function is available during computer-based exams.

CREDIT RECOMMENDATIONS

The American Council on Education's College Credit Recommendation Service (ACE CREDIT) has evaluated the DSST test development process and content of this exam. It has made the following recommendations:

Area or Course Equivalent: Computing and Information Technology
Level: Lower-level baccalaureate
Amount of Credit: 3 Semester Hours
Minimum Score: 400

EXAM CONTENT OUTLINE

The following is an outline of the content areas covered in the examination. The approximate percentage of the examination devoted to each content area is also noted.

I. **Computer Organization and Hardware – 20%**
   a. Processing components (e.g. CPU, ALU, Fetch, Execute Cycle)
   b. Primary storage (e.g. RAM, ROM, cache, virtual memory)
   c. Peripherals (e.g secondary storage, disk storage, I/O devices [RFID, biometrics, printers and scanners], communication hardware, cloud computing)
   d. Architectures (e.g. personal computers, workstations, mainframes, mobile devices)
   e. Data representation (e.g. binary system [bits, bytes], words, numbering systems, coding systems, graphic and multimedia formats)
   f. Units of measurement
      (e.g. kilobytes, gigabytes, terabytes, megahertz, gigahertz, microseconds, nanoseconds, bands, bps)

II. **Systems Software – 10%**
   a. Operating systems (e.g Windows, Apple, Android, Linux, Unix, Mainframe etc., resource allocations, job scheduling, file management, virtual computing)
   b. Utilities (e.g. virus protection/detection, backup, disk maintenance and recovery, print)
   c. User interfaces (e.g. command line, menu-driven, graphical, voice, touch, gesture)

III. **Application Software – 20%**
   a. Word processing and desktop publishing
   b. Spreadsheets (e.g. charts, graphs, functions)
   c. Presentation software including hypertext

d. Personal communications (e.g. electronic mail, list servers, chat groups, newsgroups, conferencing software, social media)
   e. Multimedia (e.g. video, audio)
   f. Databases
      a. Levels of hierarchy (e.g. fields, records, files)
      b. Database models (e.g. relational, network, hierarchical, object, data access mechanisms)
      c. Data mining/analytics
   g. Graphics (e.g. draw, paint, CAD, image processing)
   h. Software Licensing (e.g. shareware, freeware, enterprise, open source, software as a service)
   i. Commercial application software

IV. Data Communications and Networks – 20%
   a. World Wide Web (e.g. browsers, HTML, applets, search engines)
   b. Network access (e.g. file transfer, TELNET, internet service providers [ISPs])
   c. Network architectures (e.g. local area networks, wide area networks, client server, peer-to-peer, network topology, domains, routers, switches, hubs)
   d. Data communications (e.g. infrastructure, protocol [http/https])
   e. Safety and security (e.g. firewalls, IDS/IPS, hardware aspects, encryption schemes, identity and access management)
   f. Mobile networks (wireless)

V. Software Development – 10%
   a. Software life cycle (e.g. analysis, design, development, debugging, testing, maintenance)
   b. Programming methodology (e.g. procedural, object oriented)
   c. Software development tools (e.g. assemblers, profilers, debuggers, editors, compilers/interpreters)

VI. Social Impact and History – 20%
   a. History (e.g. significant people, machines and events; digital revolution, Internet, evolution of user interfaces, new applications of information technology [car, airplanes etc.])
   b. Ethical/legal issues (e.g. privacy concerns, intellectual property rights, telecommunications law, accessibility)
   c. Safety and security (e.g. hacking, malware, system access, privacy in on-line services, identity theft)
   d. Careers in Computer Science and Information Systems (e.g. growth, trends, telecommuting, compensation)
   e. Social issues (e.g. social media responsibility/etiquette [professionally and personally], artificial intelligence, globalization [off shoring], legal implications).

REFERENCES

Below is a list of reference publications that were either used as a reference to create the exam, or were used as textbooks in college courses of the same or similar title at the time the test was developed. You may reference either the current edition of these titles or textbooks currently used at a local college or university for the same class title. It is recommended that you reference more than one textbook on the topics outlined in this fact sheet.

You should begin by checking textbook content against the content outline provided before selecting textbooks that cover the test content from which to study.

Sources for study material are suggested but not limited to the following:

1. *New Perspectives on Computer Concepts*, 17th Edition-Comprehensive, 2014, June Jamrich Parsons and Dan Oja, Cengage.

2. *Using Information Technology: A Practical Introduction to Computers & Communications*, Eleventh Edition, 2015, Brian Williams and Stacey Sawyer, McGraw-Hill.

SAMPLE QUESTIONS

All test questions are in a multiple-choice format, with one correct answer and three incorrect options. The following are samples of the types of questions that may appear on the exam.

1. Which supports the largest number of users simultaneously?
   a. Personal computer
   b. Workstation
   c. Graphics terminal
   d. Mainframe

2. What is the term for a utility program that is used to make a copy of all the files on a disk?
   a. Backup
   b. Defragmenter
   c. Formatter
   d. Translator

3. What is the term for a computer that processes requests from other computers to access a data base?
   a. Client
   b. Data warehouse
   c. Server
   d. Router

4. Which stage of the software life cycle usually requires the most time and effort?
   a. Design
   b. Requirements analysis
   c. Maintenance
   d. Coding

5. The first electronic digital computer was produced in the
   a. 1920s
   b. 1940s
   c. 1960s
   d. 1980s

6. What is a mechanism that prevents unauthorized access to computers that reside on a network?
   a. Sniffer
   b. Spoofer
   c. Firewall
   d. Ethernet

Answers to sample questions:
1-D; 2-A; 3-C; 4-C; 5-B; 6- C.

HOW TO TAKE A TEST

You have studied long, hard and conscientiously.

With your official admission card in hand, and your heart pounding, you have been admitted to the examination room.

You note that there are several hundred other applicants in the examination room waiting to take the same test.

They all appear to be equally well prepared.

You know that nothing but your best effort will suffice. The "moment of truth" is at hand: you now have to demonstrate objectively, in writing, your knowledge of content and your understanding of subject matter.

You are fighting the most important battle of your life—to pass and/or score high on an examination which will determine your career and provide the economic basis for your livelihood.

What extra, special things should you know and should you do in taking the examination?

I. YOU MUST PASS AN EXAMINATION

A. WHAT EVERY CANDIDATE SHOULD KNOW
Examination applicants often ask us for help in preparing for the written test. What can I study in advance? What kinds of questions will be asked? How will the test be given? How will the papers be graded?

B. HOW ARE EXAMS DEVELOPED?
Examinations are carefully written by trained technicians who are specialists in the field known as "psychological measurement," in consultation with recognized authorities in the field of work that the test will cover. These experts recommend the subject matter areas or skills to be tested; only those knowledges or skills important to your success on the job are included. The most reliable books and source materials available are used as references. Together, the experts and technicians judge the difficulty level of the questions.
Test technicians know how to phrase questions so that the problem is clearly stated. Their ethics do not permit "trick" or "catch" questions. Questions may have been tried out on sample groups, or subjected to statistical analysis, to determine their usefulness.
Written tests are often used in combination with performance tests, ratings of training and experience, and oral interviews. All of these measures combine to form the best-known means of finding the right person for the right job.

II. HOW TO PASS THE WRITTEN TEST

A. BASIC STEPS

1) Study the announcement

How, then, can you know what subjects to study? Our best answer is: "Learn as much as possible about the class of positions for which you've applied." The exam will test the knowledge, skills and abilities needed to do the work.

Your most valuable source of information about the position you want is the official exam announcement. This announcement lists the training and experience qualifications. Check these standards and apply only if you come reasonably close to meeting them. Many jurisdictions preview the written test in the exam announcement by including a section called "Knowledge and Abilities Required," "Scope of the Examination," or some similar heading. Here you will find out specifically what fields will be tested.

2) Choose appropriate study materials

If the position for which you are applying is technical or advanced, you will read more advanced, specialized material. If you are already familiar with the basic principles of your field, elementary textbooks would waste your time. Concentrate on advanced textbooks and technical periodicals. Think through the concepts and review difficult problems in your field.

These are all general sources. You can get more ideas on your own initiative, following these leads. For example, training manuals and publications of the government agency which employs workers in your field can be useful, particularly for technical and professional positions. A letter or visit to the government department involved may result in more specific study suggestions, and certainly will provide you with a more definite idea of the exact nature of the position you are seeking.

3) Study this book!

III. KINDS OF TESTS

Tests are used for purposes other than measuring knowledge and ability to perform specified duties. For some positions, it is equally important to test ability to make adjustments to new situations or to profit from training. In others, basic mental abilities not dependent on information are essential. Questions which test these things may not appear as pertinent to the duties of the position as those which test for knowledge and information. Yet they are often highly important parts of a fair examination. For very general questions, it is almost impossible to help you direct your study efforts. What we can do is to point out some of the more common of these general abilities needed in public service positions and describe some typical questions.

1) General information

Broad, general information has been found useful for predicting job success in some kinds of work. This is tested in a variety of ways, from vocabulary lists to questions about current events. Basic background in some field of work, such as sociology or economics, may be sampled in a group of questions. Often these are principles which have become familiar to most persons through exposure rather than through formal training. It is difficult to advise you how to study for these questions; being alert to the world around you is our best suggestion.

2) Verbal ability

An example of an ability needed in many positions is verbal or language ability. Verbal ability is, in brief, the ability to use and understand words. Vocabulary and grammar tests are typical measures of this ability. Reading comprehension or paragraph interpretation questions are common in many kinds of civil service tests. You are given a paragraph of written material and asked to find its central meaning.

IV. KINDS OF QUESTIONS

1. Multiple-choice Questions

Most popular of the short-answer questions is the "multiple choice" or "best answer" question. It can be used, for example, to test for factual knowledge, ability to solve problems or judgment in meeting situations found at work.

A multiple-choice question is normally one of three types:
- It can begin with an incomplete statement followed by several possible endings. You are to find the one ending which best completes the statement, although some of the others may not be entirely wrong.
- It can also be a complete statement in the form of a question which is answered by choosing one of the statements listed.
- It can be in the form of a problem – again you select the best answer.

Here is an example of a multiple-choice question with a discussion which should give you some clues as to the method for choosing the right answer:

When an employee has a complaint about his assignment, the action which will best help him overcome his difficulty is to
- A. discuss his difficulty with his coworkers
- B. take the problem to the head of the organization
- C. take the problem to the person who gave him the assignment
- D. say nothing to anyone about his complaint

In answering this question, you should study each of the choices to find which is best. Consider choice "A" – Certainly an employee may discuss his complaint with fellow employees, but no change or improvement can result, and the complaint remains unresolved. Choice "B" is a poor choice since the head of the organization probably does not know what assignment you have been given, and taking your problem to him is known as "going over the head" of the supervisor. The supervisor, or person who made the assignment, is the person who can clarify it or correct any injustice. Choice "C" is, therefore, correct. To say nothing, as in choice "D," is unwise. Supervisors have and interest in knowing the problems employees are facing, and the employee is seeking a solution to his problem.

2. True/False

3. Matching Questions

Matching an answer from a column of choices within another column.

V. RECORDING YOUR ANSWERS

Computer terminals are used more and more today for many different kinds of exams.

For an examination with very few applicants, you may be told to record your answers in the test booklet itself. Separate answer sheets are much more common. If this separate answer sheet is to be scored by machine – and this is often the case – it is highly important that you mark your answers correctly in order to get credit.

VI. BEFORE THE TEST

YOUR PHYSICAL CONDITION IS IMPORTANT

If you are not well, you can't do your best work on tests. If you are half asleep, you can't do your best either. Here are some tips:

1) Get about the same amount of sleep you usually get. Don't stay up all night before the test, either partying or worrying—DON'T DO IT!
2) If you wear glasses, be sure to wear them when you go to take the test. This goes for hearing aids, too.
3) If you have any physical problems that may keep you from doing your best, be sure to tell the person giving the test. If you are sick or in poor health, you relay cannot do your best on any test. You can always come back and take the test some other time.

Common sense will help you find procedures to follow to get ready for an examination. Too many of us, however, overlook these sensible measures. Indeed, nervousness and fatigue have been found to be the most serious reasons why applicants fail to do their best on civil service tests. Here is a list of reminders:

- Begin your preparation early – Don't wait until the last minute to go scurrying around for books and materials or to find out what the position is all about.
- Prepare continuously – An hour a night for a week is better than an all-night cram session. This has been definitely established. What is more, a night a week for a month will return better dividends than crowding your study into a shorter period of time.
- Locate the place of the exam – You have been sent a notice telling you when and where to report for the examination. If the location is in a different town or otherwise unfamiliar to you, it would be well to inquire the best route and learn something about the building.
- Relax the night before the test – Allow your mind to rest. Do not study at all that night. Plan some mild recreation or diversion; then go to bed early and get a good night's sleep.
- Get up early enough to make a leisurely trip to the place for the test – This way unforeseen events, traffic snarls, unfamiliar buildings, etc. will not upset you.
- Dress comfortably – A written test is not a fashion show. You will be known by number and not by name, so wear something comfortable.
- Leave excess paraphernalia at home – Shopping bags and odd bundles will get in your way. You need bring only the items mentioned in the official notice you received; usually everything you need is provided. Do not bring reference books to the exam. They will only confuse those last minutes and be taken away from you when in the test room.

- Arrive somewhat ahead of time – If because of transportation schedules you must get there very early, bring a newspaper or magazine to take your mind off yourself while waiting.
- Locate the examination room – When you have found the proper room, you will be directed to the seat or part of the room where you will sit. Sometimes you are given a sheet of instructions to read while you are waiting. Do not fill out any forms until you are told to do so; just read them and be prepared.
- Relax and prepare to listen to the instructions
- If you have any physical problem that may keep you from doing your best, be sure to tell the test administrator. If you are sick or in poor health, you really cannot do your best on the exam. You can come back and take the test some other time.

VII. AT THE TEST

The day of the test is here and you have the test booklet in your hand. The temptation to get going is very strong. Caution! There is more to success than knowing the right answers. You must know how to identify your papers and understand variations in the type of short-answer question used in this particular examination. Follow these suggestions for maximum results from your efforts:

1) Cooperate with the monitor

The test administrator has a duty to create a situation in which you can be as much at ease as possible. He will give instructions, tell you when to begin, check to see that you are marking your answer sheet correctly, and so on. He is not there to guard you, although he will see that your competitors do not take unfair advantage. He wants to help you do your best.

2) Listen to all instructions

Don't jump the gun! Wait until you understand all directions. In most civil service tests you get more time than you need to answer the questions. So don't be in a hurry. Read each word of instructions until you clearly understand the meaning. Study the examples, listen to all announcements and follow directions. Ask questions if you do not understand what to do.

3) Identify your papers

Civil service exams are usually identified by number only. You will be assigned a number; you must not put your name on your test papers. Be sure to copy your number correctly. Since more than one exam may be given, copy your exact examination title.

4) Plan your time

Unless you are told that a test is a "speed" or "rate of work" test, speed itself is usually not important. Time enough to answer all the questions will be provided, but this does not mean that you have all day. An overall time limit has been set. Divide the total time (in minutes) by the number of questions to determine the approximate time you have for each question.

5) Do not linger over difficult questions

If you come across a difficult question, mark it with a paper clip (useful to have along) and come back to it when you have been through the booklet. One caution if you do this – be sure to skip a number on your answer sheet as well. Check often to be sure that you have not lost your place and that you are marking in the row numbered the same as the question you are answering.

6) Read the questions
    Be sure you know what the question asks! Many capable people are unsuccessful because they failed to read the questions correctly.

7) Answer all questions
    Unless you have been instructed that a penalty will be deducted for incorrect answers, it is better to guess than to omit a question.

8) Speed tests
    It is often better NOT to guess on speed tests. It has been found that on timed tests people are tempted to spend the last few seconds before time is called in marking answers at random – without even reading them – in the hope of picking up a few extra points. To discourage this practice, the instructions may warn you that your score will be "corrected" for guessing. That is, a penalty will be applied. The incorrect answers will be deducted from the correct ones, or some other penalty formula will be used.

9) Review your answers
    If you finish before time is called, go back to the questions you guessed or omitted to give them further thought. Review other answers if you have time.

10) Return your test materials
    If you are ready to leave before others have finished or time is called, take ALL your materials to the monitor and leave quietly. Never take any test material with you. The monitor can discover whose papers are not complete, and taking a test booklet may be grounds for disqualification.

VIII. EXAMINATION TECHNIQUES

1) Read the general instructions carefully. These are usually printed on the first page of the exam booklet. As a rule, these instructions refer to the timing of the examination; the fact that you should not start work until the signal and must stop work at a signal, etc. If there are any special instructions, such as a choice of questions to be answered, make sure that you note this instruction carefully.

2) When you are ready to start work on the examination, that is as soon as the signal has been given, read the instructions to each question booklet, underline any key words or phrases, such as least, best, outline, describe and the like. In this way you will tend to answer as requested rather than discover on reviewing your paper that you listed without describing, that you selected the worst choice rather than the best choice, etc.

3) If the examination is of the objective or multiple-choice type – that is, each question will also give a series of possible answers: A, B, C or D, and you are called upon to select the best answer and write the letter next to that answer on your answer paper – it is advisable to start answering each question in turn. There may be anywhere from 50 to 100 such questions in the three or four hours allotted and you can see how much time would be taken if you read through all the questions before beginning to answer any. Furthermore, if you

come across a question or group of questions which you know would be difficult to answer, it would undoubtedly affect your handling of all the other questions.

4) If the examination is of the essay type and contains but a few questions, it is a moot point as to whether you should read all the questions before starting to answer any one. Of course, if you are given a choice – say five out of seven and the like – then it is essential to read all the questions so you can eliminate the two that are most difficult. If, however, you are asked to answer all the questions, there may be danger in trying to answer the easiest one first because you may find that you will spend too much time on it. The best technique is to answer the first question, then proceed to the second, etc.

5) Time your answers. Before the exam begins, write down the time it started, then add the time allowed for the examination and write down the time it must be completed, then divide the time available somewhat as follows:
    - If 3-1/2 hours are allowed, that would be 210 minutes. If you have 80 objective-type questions, that would be an average of 2-1/2 minutes per question. Allow yourself no more than 2 minutes per question, or a total of 160 minutes, which will permit about 50 minutes to review.
    - If for the time allotment of 210 minutes there are 7 essay questions to answer, that would average about 30 minutes a question. Give yourself only 25 minutes per question so that you have about 35 minutes to review.

6) The most important instruction is to read each question and make sure you know what is wanted. The second most important instruction is to time yourself properly so that you answer every question. The third most important instruction is to answer every question. Guess if you have to but include something for each question. Remember that you will receive no credit for a blank and will probably receive some credit if you write something in answer to an essay question. If you guess a letter – say "B" for a multiple-choice question – you may have guessed right. If you leave a blank as an answer to a multiple-choice question, the examiners may respect your feelings but it will not add a point to your score. Some exams may penalize you for wrong answers, so in such cases only, you may not want to guess unless you have some basis for your answer.

7) Suggestions
    a. Objective-type questions
        1. Examine the question booklet for proper sequence of pages and questions
        2. Read all instructions carefully
        3. Skip any question which seems too difficult; return to it after all other questions have been answered
        4. Apportion your time properly; do not spend too much time on any single question or group of questions
        5. Note and underline key words – all, most, fewest, least, best, worst, same, opposite, etc.
        6. Pay particular attention to negatives
        7. Note unusual option, e.g., unduly long, short, complex, different or similar in content to the body of the question
        8. Observe the use of "hedging" words – probably, may, most likely, etc.

9. Make sure that your answer is put next to the same number as the question
10. Do not second-guess unless you have good reason to believe the second answer is definitely more correct
11. Cross out original answer if you decide another answer is more accurate; do not erase until you are ready to hand your paper in
12. Answer all questions; guess unless instructed otherwise
13. Leave time for review

b. Essay questions
   1. Read each question carefully
   2. Determine exactly what is wanted. Underline key words or phrases.
   3. Decide on outline or paragraph answer
   4. Include many different points and elements unless asked to develop any one or two points or elements
   5. Show impartiality by giving pros and cons unless directed to select one side only
   6. Make and write down any assumptions you find necessary to answer the questions
   7. Watch your English, grammar, punctuation and choice of words
   8. Time your answers; don't crowd material

8) Answering the essay question

Most essay questions can be answered by framing the specific response around several key words or ideas. Here are a few such key words or ideas:

M's: manpower, materials, methods, money, management
P's: purpose, program, policy, plan, procedure, practice, problems, pitfalls, personnel, public relations

a. Six basic steps in handling problems:
   1. Preliminary plan and background development
   2. Collect information, data and facts
   3. Analyze and interpret information, data and facts
   4. Analyze and develop solutions as well as make recommendations
   5. Prepare report and sell recommendations
   6. Install recommendations and follow up effectiveness

b. Pitfalls to avoid
   1. Taking things for granted – A statement of the situation does not necessarily imply that each of the elements is necessarily true; for example, a complaint may be invalid and biased so that all that can be taken for granted is that a complaint has been registered
   2. Considering only one side of a situation – Wherever possible, indicate several alternatives and then point out the reasons you selected the best one
   3. Failing to indicate follow up – Whenever your answer indicates action on your part, make certain that you will take proper follow-up action to see how successful your recommendations, procedures or actions turn out to be
   4. Taking too long in answering any single question – Remember to time your answers properly

EXAMINATION SECTION

EXAMINATION SECTION
TEST 1

DIRECTIONS: Each question or incomplete statement is followed by several suggested answers or completions. Select the one that BEST answers the question or completes the statement. *PRINT THE LETTER OF THE CORRECT ANSWER IN THE SPACE AT THE RIGHT.*

1. Which one of the following is considered a word processor program? 1.____
   A. Microsoft Word
   B. Microsoft Works
   C. Notepad
   D. Both A and B

2. Default headings are available under the _____ tab. 2.____
   A. Insert   B. Home   C. File   D. View

3. _____ deals with font, alignment and margins. 3.____
   A. Selecting   B. Formatting   C. Composing   D. Pattern

4. Which one of the following is the BEST format for storing bit-mapped images on the computer? 4.____
   A. .JPG   B. .PNG   C. .GIF   D. .TIF

5. A header specifies an area in the _____ margins of every page. 5.____
   A. top   B. bottom   C. left   D. right

6. When an Excel file is inserted into a Word document, the data is 6.____
   A. hyperlinked
   B. placed in a Word table
   C. linked
   D. embedded

7. A workbook in Excel is a file that 7.____
   A. is primarily used to generate graphs
   B. is often used for word processing
   C. can contain many sheets, chart sheets and worksheets
   D. both A and B

8. Excel can produce chart types that include 8.____
   A. only line graphs
   B. bar charts, line graphs and pie charts
   C. line graphs and pie charts only
   D. bar charts and line graphs only

9. In PowerPoint, the motion path is a 9.____
   A. method of moving items on the slide
   B. method of advancing slides
   C. indentation
   D. type of animation

1

10. _____ replaces similar words in a document.
    A. Word Count   B. Thesaurus   C. Wrap Text   D. Format Printer

11. The MOST simple description of the Internet is
    A. a single network
    B. a huge collection of different networks
    C. collection of LANs
    D. single WAN

12. How can a computer be connected to the Internet?
    A. Through internet service providers   B. Internet society
    C. Internet architecture board   D. Local area network

13. A software program that is used to view web pages is known as a(n)
    A. Internet browser   B. interpreter
    C. operating system   D. website

14. Which of the following is used to search anything on the Internet?
    A. Search engines   B. Routers
    C. Social networks   D. Websites

15. When a website is accessed, its main page is called
    A. home page   B. back end page
    C. dead end   D. both A and B

16. Google Docs provides _____, which is a salient feature of Google Doc.
    A. image processing   B. synchronization
    C. both A and B   D. installation

17. Documents in Google Drive could be accessed from
    A. only a personal computer
    B. any computer that has Internet connection
    C. only that computer that has Google drive on hard disk
    D. both B and C

18. In an email address, for example test@gmail.com, "gmail" is known as
    A. domain
    B. host computer in commercial domain
    C. internet service provider
    D. URL

19. Which of the following is NOT a well-known domain?
    A. .edu   B. .com   C. .org   D. .army

20. Cyberspace is an alternative name used for
    A. Internet   B. information   C. virtual space   D. data space

21. Which one of the following is NOT an Internet browser?
    A. Chrome   B. Firefly   C. Firefox   D. Safari

22. Which of the following is NOT a past or current search engine?   22.____
    A. Apple   B. Lycos   C. Bing   D. Google

23. Document scanning could be done through   23.____
    A. OCR   B. OMR
    C. both A and B   D. dot-matrix printer

24. _____ are used to fill out empty fields in scanned images of data.   24.____
    A. Computerized optical scanners   B. OCR software
    C. Scanners   D. Laser printers

25. All of the following are examples of hardware for standard home use EXCEPT   25.____
    A. flash drives   B. inkjet printers
    C. servers   D. laser printers

KEY (CORRECT ANSWERS)

1.	D		11.	B
2.	B		12.	A
3.	B		13.	A
4.	D		14.	A
5.	A		15.	A
6.	B		16.	B
7.	C		17.	B
8.	B		18.	B
9.	A		19.	D
10.	B		20.	A

21. B
22. A
23. C
24. A
25. C

TEST 2

DIRECTIONS: Each question or incomplete statement is followed by several suggested answers or completions. Select the one that BEST answers the question or completes the statement. *PRINT THE LETTER OF THE CORRECT ANSWER IN THE SPACE AT THE RIGHT.*

1. In a spreadsheet, data is organized in the form of
   A. lines and spaces
   B. rows and columns
   C. layers and planes
   D. height and width

   1.____

2. Which one of the following menus is used to protect a worksheet?
   A. Edit
   B. Format
   C. Data
   D. Tools

   2.____

3. _____ corrects spelling mistakes automatically.
   A. Word wrap
   B. AutoCorrect
   C. Spell checker
   D. Thesaurus

   3.____

4. Which function is used to automatically align text?
   A. Justification
   B. Indentation
   C. Both A and B
   D. None of the above

   4.____

5. Orientation is the property of the _____ function.
   A. Print
   B. Design
   C. Image
   D. Both A and B

   5.____

6. Special effects that are used to present slides in a presentation are known as
   A. effects
   B. custom animation
   C. transition
   D. present animation

   6.____

7. Page setup and print functions can typically be found in the ____ menu.
   A. tools
   B. format
   C. file
   D. edit

   7.____

8. Which one of the following is considered removable storage media?
   A. Scanner
   B. Flash drive
   C. External hard drive
   D. Both B and C

   8.____

9. Which component of the computer is called the brain of the computer?
   A. ALU
   B. Memory
   C. Control Unit
   D. CPU

   9.____

10. .txt is a file that is named for _____ files.
    A. Notepad
    B. Word
    C. Paint
    D. Excel

    10.____

11. Software programs that are automatically downloaded and work within a browser are known as
    A. plug-in
    B. utilities
    C. widgets
    D. add-on

    11.____

12. _____ is a computer that requests data from other computers on the Internet.
    A. Client
    B. Server
    C. Super computer
    D. Personal computer

13. A wizard is considered as a _____ file with prompt display.
    A. system   B. program   C. help   D. application

14. E-mails from unknown senders go into the _____ folder.
    A. Spam   B. Trash   C. Drafts   D. Inbox

15. LAN is an abbreviation for _____ area network.
    A. line   B. local   C. large   D. limited

16. Which of the following is NOT an extension for an image file?
    A. .bmp   B. .jpg   C. .png   D. .xls

17. In the e-mail address *test@gmail.com*, "test" is the _____ name.
    A. domain   B. user   C. server   D. ISP

18. To e-mail multiple recipients while hiding the recipients from view, use the ___ function.
    A. BCC   B. CC   C. send   D. hide

19. The system that translates an IP address into a simple form that is easy to remember is
    A. domain name system
    B. domain
    C. domain numbering system
    D. server domain

20. Which one of the following is the CORRECT method to send a file through e-mail?
    A. CC
    B. Attachment
    C. Embed through HTML
    D. Both A and B

21. Inkjet printers are categorized as a(n) _____ printer.
    A. character   B. ink   C. line   D. band

22. Which one of the following is a storage medium that has a shape of a circular plate?
    A. Disk   B. CPU   C. ALU   D. Printer

23. Ctrl+P activates the _____ function.
    A. reboot   B. save   C. print   D. paint

24. The file extension .exe represents an _____ file.
    A. examination   B. extra   C. executable   D. extension

25. Which of the following is NOT considered an input device? 25.____
    A. OCR   B. Optical scanner
    C. Printer   D. Keyboard

KEY (CORRECT ANSWERS)

1. B
2. D
3. B
4. A
5. A

6. C
7. C
8. D
9. D
10. A

11. B
12. A
13. C
14. A
15. B

16. D
17. B
18. A
19. A
20. B

21. C
22. A
23. C
24. C
25. C

TEST 3

DIRECTIONS: Each question or incomplete statement is followed by several suggested answers or completions. Select the one that BEST answers the question or completes the statement. *PRINT THE LETTER OF THE CORRECT ANSWER IN THE SPACE AT THE RIGHT.*

1. Excel is a _____ program.
   A. graphics
   B. word processor
   C. spreadsheet
   D. typewriter

   1.____

2. Basically, a word processor program like Microsoft Word is a replacement for
   A. manual work
   B. typewriters
   C. both A and B
   D. graphical programs

   2.____

3. Which one of the following could be added as a sound effect to a PowerPoint presentation?
   A. .wav files and .mid files
   B. .wav files and .gif files
   C. .wav files and .jpg files
   D. .jpg files and .gif files

   3.____

4. Google Drive is an example of _____ software.
   A. system   B. application   C. database   D. firmware

   4.____

5. PDF stands for _____ document format.
   A. portable   B. picture   C. plain   D. private

   5.____

6. Which one of the following is an example of internal memory of a computer?
   A. Disks   B. Pen drive   C. RAM   D. CDs

   6.____

7. A keyboard is an example of a(n) _____ device.
   A. input
   B. output
   C. word processor
   D. printing

   7.____

8. Clip art is a collection of _____ that can be inserted into a document.
   A. text files
   B. image files
   C. templates
   D. audio files

   8.____

9. _____ is a distinctive part of memory which holds the contents temporarily during cut or copy functions.
   A. Clipboard   B. Macro   C. Template   D. Clip art

   9.____

10. _____ is a process to store files on a computer from the Internet.
    A. Uploading
    B. Downloading
    C. Pulling
    D. Transferring

    10.____

11. "Cut and paste" refers to
    A. deleting and moving text
    B. restoring and updating software
    C. cleaning images
    D. replacing images

    11.____

12. Which one of the following is a compressed format for images?
    A. GIF B. JPGE C. PNG D. JPG

13. A computer stores information and data inside the
    A. hard drive B. CPU C. CD D. monitor

14. WWW is an abbreviation of
    A. world wide web
    B. wide world web
    C. web worldwide
    D. world wide website

15. A _____ computer holds more than one processor.
    A. multithread
    B. multi-unit
    C. multiprocessor
    D. multiprogramming

16. Landscape and portrait are properties of
    A. page layout B. design C. formatting D. text

17. _____ includes the company's name, address, phone number and e-mail address.
    A. Letterhead B. Template C. Visiting Card D. Brochure

18. _____ Server provides database services for other computers.
    A. Application B. Web C. Database D. FTP

19. Which one of the following is responsible for storing movies, images and pictures?
    A. File server
    B. Web server
    C. Database server
    D. Application server

20. GUI stands for graphical
    A. user interface
    B. unified instrument
    C. unified interface
    D. user instrument

21. Scanner is an example of a(n) _____ device.
    A. output B. input C. printing D. both A and B

22. Which one of the following is NOT an example of computer hardware?
    A. Printer B. Scanner C. Mouse D. Antivirus

23. Which one of the following provides the BEST quality reproduction of graphics?
    A. Laser printer
    B. Inkjet printer
    C. Dot-matrix printer
    D. Plotter

24. If an e-mail sender is unknown, then do not download the _____ because it might contain a virus.
    A. attachment
    B. email
    C. spam
    D. both A and B

3 (#3)

25. The BEST way to send identical emails to more than one person is to 25.____
    A. use the CC option
    B. add email ID to address
    C. forward
    D. both A and B

KEY (CORRECT ANSWERS)

1. C
2. B
3. A
4. B
5. A

6. C
7. A
8. B
9. A
10. B

11. A
12. A
13. A
14. A
15. C

16. A
17. A
18. C
19. A
20. A

21. B
22. D
23. D
24. A
25. A

TEST 4

DIRECTIONS: Each question or incomplete statement is followed by several suggested answers or completions. Select the one that BEST answers the question or completes the statement. *PRINT THE LETTER OF THE CORRECT ANSWER IN THE SPACE AT THE RIGHT.*

1. A keyboard shortcut for saving files is
   A. Alt+S   B. Ctrl+S   C. Ctrl+SV   D. S+Enter

2. Which of the following is NOT a term relevant to Excel?
   A. slide
   B. cell
   C. formula
   D. column

3. A _____ background is a grainy and non-smooth surface.
   A. texture   B. gradient   C. solid   D. pattern

4. Word wrap forces all text to fit within the defined
   A. margin   B. indent   C. block   D. box

5. In Microsoft Word, overview of the prepared document could be better seen through
   A. Preview
   B. Print Preview
   C. Review
   D. both A and B

6. The amount of vertical space between text line in a document is known as
   A. double space
   B. line spacing
   C. single space
   D. vertical spacing

7. Which one of the following devices is required for Internet connection?
   A. Joy stick   B. Modem   C. NIC card   D. Optical drive

8. IBM is a short form used for
   A. Internal Business Management
   B. International Business Management
   C. Internal Business Machines
   D. International Business Machines

9. Which one of the following is static and non-volatile memory?
   A. RAM   B. ROM   C. BIOS   D. Cache

10. One disadvantage of Google Docs is
    A. less storage
    B. compatibility
    C. needs connectivity to Internet
    D. synchronization

11. WAN is an abbreviation of _____ area network.
    A. wide   B. wired   C. whole   D. while

12. Bibliography can be created through the _____ tab.
    A. References   B. Design   C. Review   D. Insert

13. The _____ is MOST likely shared in a computer network.
    A. keyboard   B. speaker   C. printer   D. scanner

14. A normal computer is not able to boot if it does not have a(n)
    A. operating system   B. complier
    C. loader   D. assembler

15. _____ is another name for junk e-mails.
    A. Spam   B. Spoof   C. Spool   D. Sniffer scripts

16. A table of contents can be created automatically by using an option in
    A. Page Layout   B. Insert   C. References   D. View

17. ALU stands for
    A. arithmetic logic unit   B. array logic unit
    C. application logic unit   D. both A and B

18. Orientation is concerned with the _____ set-up of the page.
    A. horizontal   B. vertical   C. both A and B   D. spacing

19. _____ is a form of written communication within the same company which comprises guide words as heading.
    A. Memorandum   B. Letterhead
    C. Template   D. None of the above

20. Which one of the following is NOT a web browser?
    A. Chrome   B. Opera   C. Firefox   D. Drupal

21. .net domain is specifically used for
    A. international organization
    B. internet infrastructure and service providers
    C. educational institutes
    D. commercial business

22. A modem is not required when the Internet is connected through
    A. Wi-Fi   B. LAN
    C. dial-up phone   D. cable

23. Mail Merge uses _____ to create separate copies of a document for multiple people in Microsoft Word.
    A. primary document   B. data document
    C. both A and B   D. web page

24. Linux is an example of
    A. operating system   B. malware
    C. firmware   D. application program

25. Which one of the following is a CORRECT format for a website address?   25._____
    A. www@com
    B. www.test.com
    C. www.test25A@com
    D. www#TeST.com

KEY (CORRECT ANSWERS)

1. B
2. A
3. B
4. A
5. B

6. B
7. B
8. D
9. B
10. C

11. A
12. A
13. C
14. A
15. A

16. C
17. A
18. C
19. A
20. D

21. B
22. A
23. C
24. A
25. B

EXAMINATION SECTION
TEST 1

DIRECTIONS: Each question or incomplete statement is followed by several suggested answers or completions. Select the one that BEST answers the question or completes the statement. *PRINT THE LETTER OF THE CORRECT ANSWER IN THE SPACE AT THE RIGHT.*

1. What is the default compressing software of Windows?
   A. WinRar
   B. 7-zip
   C. WinZip
   D. All of the above

   1.____

2. Which software does NOT require special drives to run?
   A. Mouse
   B. Keyboard
   C. Joystick
   D. All of the above

   2.____

3. What software is required to run PDF?
   A. MS Word
   B. Windows Media Player
   C. Adobe Photoshop
   D. Adobe Reader

   3.____

4. An error message that says "there is a problem with this website's security certificate" appears when
   A. Windows is outdated
   B. browser is outdated
   C. date and time are wrong
   D. internet is disabled

   4.____

5. Software should always be _____ for better performance.
   A. disabled
   B. updated
   C. uninstalled
   D. all of the above

   5.____

6. SATA is the abbreviation for
   A. Sequential Advanced Technology Advancement
   B. Serial Advanced Technology Attachment
   C. Serial Automatic Technology Attachment
   D. Supper Advanced Technology Attachment

   6.____

7. Which of the following is a part of management software development?
   A. People
   B. Product
   C. Process
   D. All of the above

   7.____

8. _____ is a tool in the design phase.
   A. Abstraction
   B. Refinement
   C. Information Hiding
   D. All of the above

   8.____

9. What is the other name used for white box software testing technique?
   A. Basic Path
   B. Graph Testing
   C. Data Flow
   D. Glass Box Testing

   9.____

13

10. _____ is included in the Turnkey package.
    A. Software B. Hardware
    C. Training D. All of the above

    10._____

11. _____ are types of a record access method.
    A. Sequential and random B. Direct and immediate
    C. Sequential and indexed D. Online and real time

    11._____

12. _____ has a sequential file organization.
    A. Grocery store checkout B. Bank checking account
    C. Payroll D. Airline reservation

    12._____

13. What will you recommend when users are involved in complex tasks?
    A. A short term memory B. Demands on shortcut usage
    C. Both A and B D. None of the above

    13._____

14. _____ protocols are similar to HTTP.
    A. FTP; SMTP B. FTP; SNMP
    C. FTP; MTV D. SMTP; SNMP

    14._____

15. _____ is the oldest data model.
    A. Relational B. Deductive
    C. Physical D. Hierarchical

    15._____

16. _____ defines the transaction executed.
    A. Committed B. Aborted
    C. Failed D. Rolled Back

    16._____

17. _____ is NOT a deadlock managing strategy.
    A. Deadlock prevention B. Timeout
    C. Deadlock detection D. Deadlock annihilation

    17._____

18. _____ is the average execution time of the monitor power process.
    A. 1 ms B. 10 ms
    C. 100 ms D. None of the above

    18._____

19. _____ is NOT a dimension of scalability.
    A. Size B. Distribution
    C. Interception D. Manageability

    19._____

20. What would you do if the icons on the desktop are white or missing colors?
    A. End the explorer.exe B. Check settings in Appearance
    C. Both A and B D. None of the above

    20._____

21. What would you do if while using AutoCAD you receive a message of "license is invalid"?
    A. Delete licensing file B. Re-enter registration information
    C. Both A and B D. None of the above

    21._____

22. What would you do to satisfy the growing communication need in your company? 22.____
    A. Use front end processor
    B. Use a multiplexer
    C. Use a controller
    D. All of the above

23. _____ is a part of x.25. 23.____
    A. Technique for start stop data
    B. Technique for dial access
    C. DTE/DCE interface
    D. None of the above

24. Which of the following is a software product? 24.____
    A. CAD, Cam
    B. Firmware, Embedded
    C. Generic, Customized
    D. Both A and B

25. ACT in Boehm software maintenance model is the abbreviation for 25.____
    A. Actual Change Track
    B. Annual Change Track
    C. Annual Change Traffic
    D. Actual Change Traffic

KEY (CORRECT ANSWERS)

1.	C	11.	A
2.	D	12.	B
3.	D	13.	A
4.	C	14.	A
5.	B	15.	D
6.	B	16.	A
7.	D	17.	D
8.	D	18.	A
9.	D	19.	D
10.	D	20.	C

21.	C
22.	D
23.	C
24.	C
25.	C

TEST 2

DIRECTIONS: Each question or incomplete statement is followed by several suggested answers or completions. Select the one that BEST answers the question or completes the statement. *PRINT THE LETTER OF THE CORRECT ANSWER IN THE SPACE AT THE RIGHT.*

1. Software maintenance incorporates
   A. Error Correction
   B. Enhancement of capabilities
   C. Deletion of obsolete capabilities
   D. All of the above

   1.____

2. Software Maintenance model called Taute has _____ number of phases.
   A. 6   B. 7   C. 8   D. 9

   2.____

3. _____ is a software process certification.
   A. JAVA certified
   B. IBM certified
   C. ISO-9000
   D. Microsoft certified

   3.____

4. _____ is known as quality management in software development.
   A. SQA
   B. SQM
   C. SQI
   D. Both A and B

   4.____

5. Software reliability means
   A. time   B. efficiency   C. quality   D. speed

   5.____

6. A software package designed to store and manage databases is
   A. Database   B. DBMS   C. Data Model   D. Data

   6.____

7.

   The above image represents a _____ relation.
   A. many to many
   B. many to one
   C. one to one
   D. one to many

   7.____

8. The diagram shown at the right indicates that
   A. there is a missing entity
   B. students attend courses
   C. many students can attend many courses
   D. students have to attend more than one course

   8.____

9. In relational algebra, the union of two sets (set A and set B) corresponds to
   A. A OR B   B. A + B   C. A AND B   D. A - B

   9.____

10. _____ is the location of the keyboard status byte.
    A. 0040:0000H   B. 0040:0013H
    C. 0040:0015H   D. 0040:0017H

11. What is the number of maximum interrupts occurring in a PC?
    A. 64   B. 128   C. 256   D. 512

12. How many bytes are there in an operating system name in the boot block?
    A. 3   B. 5   C. 8   D. 11

13. What is the size of a DPB structure?
    A. 16   B. 32   C. 64   D. 128

14. _____ is the file system in CD.
    A. Contiguous   B. Chained   C. Indexed   D. None

15. NTFS volume is accessed directly in
    A. DOS   B. Linux   C. Windows   D. MAC

16. _____.com is an MS DOS file in the boot disk.
    A. Command   B. Start   C. Tree   D. Ver

17. _____ is a table in the OS that keeps information of files.
    A. FFT   B. FIT   C. FAT   D. DIT

18. _____ is a system programming language.
    A. C   B. PL/360
    C. PASCAL   D. All of the above

19. What would you do if the icons disappear from the Taskbar?
    A. Press Windows Key + R and type "regedit"
    B. Delete Icon stream and past icon Stream values
    C. Uncheck user interface
    D. All of the above

20. What would you do if you want to make sure the drivers of the old printers are removed?
    A. Check Server Properties   B. Check settings in Appearance
    C. Both A and B   D. None of the above

21. Microsoft has introduced _____ tool that incorporates all the automated fixes.
    A. Fix It Center   B. Fix All
    C. Fixing It   D. none of the above

22. A PC can only use one _____ device at a time.
    A. Ready Boost   B. Built-in Flash
    C. RAM   D. all of the above

23. You need to edit two registry keys called _____ if you cannot customize 23._____
    folders.
    A. bagMRU and Bags
    B. RAM and ROM
    C. DTE/DCE interface
    D. none of the above

24. What would you do if your PC does not have a Windows Installation disk? 24._____
    A. Select "create a system repair" disc
    B. Place a DVD in the writeable drive
    C. Create a bootable disc by the "Repair Your Computer"
    D. All of the above

25. Code of conduct defines the 25._____
    A. employees' legal and ethical obligations
    B. commitment to integrity
    C. terms and condition of the company
    D. legal contract

KEY (CORRECT ANSWERS)

1.	D		11.	C
2.	C		12.	C
3.	C		13.	B
4.	A		14.	A
5.	A		15.	A
6.	B		16.	A
7.	D		17.	A
8.	C		18.	D
9.	B		19.	D
10.	D		20.	C

21. A
22. A
23. A
24. D
25. A

TEST 3

DIRECTIONS: Each question or incomplete statement is followed by several suggested answers or completions. Select the one that BEST answers the question or completes the statement. *PRINT THE LETTER OF THE CORRECT ANSWER IN THE SPACE AT THE RIGHT.*

1. What would you do if the drive does not open by double-clicking?
   A. Check search option in drive C
   B. Enter regsvr32/I shell32.dll in the Run
   C. Check settings in the control panel
   D. Both A and B

   1._____

2. What would you do if you attach another display unit to your PC but it remains blank?
   A. Check the cables
   B. Check display properties
   C. Select the properties to duplicate each other
   D. All of the above

   2._____

3. _____ helps you when you are locked out of Manager and Registry Editor?
   A. Virus Effect Remover   B. Fix It Tool
   C. Safe mode   D. All of the above

   3._____

4. The two types of cache memory in RAM are called
   A. ALU and CPU   B. Buffer and Procedure
   C. Date and Timing   D. DLL and STAT

   4._____

5. _____ points at the same location when the keyboard buffer is empty.
   A. Interrupt   B. Head and Tail
   C. Tail   D. All of the above

   5._____

6. _____ frequency is divided by the interval time.
   A. Output   B. Input
   C. Both A and B   D. None of the above
   E. All of the above

   6._____

7. What is the number of PPI present in a standard PC?
   A. 1   B. 4   C. 8   D. 16

   7._____

8. _____ is used as a status port of the keyboard.
   A. 64H   B. 44H
   C. 77H   D. All of the above

   8._____

9. _____ is a computer with an 80286 microprocessor.
   A. XT computer   B. PC/AT computer
   C. PS/2 computer   D. None of the above

   9._____

10. _____ is not a process.
    A. Arranging
    B. Manipulation
    C. Calculating
    D. Gathering

11. _____ is a sequential processing application.
    A. Grades processing
    B. Payroll processing
    C. Both A and B
    D. All of the above

12. _____ has a record disk address.
    A. Track Number
    B. Sector Number
    C. Surface Number
    D. All of the above

13. Which printer would you NOT use while printing on a carbon form?
    A. Daisy Wheel
    B. Dot Matrix
    C. Laser
    D. None of the above

14. A(n) _____ produces the BEST quality graphic production.
    A. laser printer
    B. inkjet printer
    C. plotter
    D. dot matrix

15. _____ allows both read and write operations at the same time.
    A. ROM
    B. RAM
    C. EPROM
    D. None of the above

16. _____ has the shortest access time.
    A. Cache Memory
    B. Magnetic Bubble Memory
    C. Magnetic Core Memory
    D. RAM

17. _____ defines the status of resources assigned to the process.
    A. Process Control
    B. ALU
    C. Register Unit
    D. Process Description

18. Memory _____ controls access to the memory.
    A. map
    B. protection
    C. management
    D. instruction

19. _____ is able to record and track all the information in a database about animal movement once placed on the animal.
    A. POS
    B. RFID
    C. PPS
    D. GPS

20. The print of a picture taken from a digital camera is said to be a(n)
    A. data
    B. output
    C. input
    D. none of the above

21. _____ are the two types of record access methods.
    A. Sequential and Random
    B. Direct and Immediate
    C. Online and Real Time
    D. None of the above

22. _____ is the most efficient method of file organization when the file is highly active.
    A. ISAM
    B. VSAM
    C. B-Tree
    D. All of the above

23. _____ is the standard approach for storing data.
    A. MIS
    B. Structured Programming
    C. CODASYL specification
    D. None of the above

24. Which of the following RDBMS supports client server application development?
    A. dBase V
    B. Oracle 7.1
    C. FoxPro 2.1
    D. Both A and B

25. Which of the following techniques would you use to find the location of the element?
    A. Traversal
    B. Search
    C. Sort
    D. None of the above

KEY (CORRECT ANSWERS)

1. D
2. D
3. A
4. B
5. B

6. B
7. B
8. A
9. B
10. D

11. C
12. D
13. C
14. C
15. B

16. A
17. D
18. A
19. B
20. B

21. A
22. A
23. C
24. B
25. B

TEST 4

DIRECTIONS: Each question or incomplete statement is followed by several suggested answers or completions. Select the one that BEST answers the question or completes the statement. *PRINT THE LETTER OF THE CORRECT ANSWER IN THE SPACE AT THE RIGHT.*

1. A band is equal to 1.____
   A. a byte
   B. a bit
   C. 100 bits
   D. none of the above

2. The number of zeroes in each symbol in an odd-parity is 2.____
   A. odd
   B. even
   D. unknown
   D. both A and B

3. _____ is also called an IPng. 3.____
   A. IPv4
   B. IPv5
   C. IPv6
   D. All of the above

4. IPv6 addresses are written in 4.____
   A. hexadecimal
   B. binary
   C. decimal
   D. none of the above

5. Green PCs are designed to 5.____
   A. minimize power consumption
   B. minimize inactive components
   C. minimize electricity bill
   D. all of the above

6. Hyper V Network Virtualizations do not have the ability to access the outside world unless you 6.____
   A. implement a forwarding agent
   B. implement a gateway
   C. implement a CISCO NEXUS
   D. None of the above
   E. All of the above

7. What would you do to create a shortcut of a website on the desktop? 7.____
   A. Left click on the icon present on the left side of the address bar and drag it to the desktop
   B. Save the webpage through the Save Page As
   C. Bookmark the page
   D. All of the above

8. E-mail, word documents, web pages, video and photos are called unstructured data because 8.____
   A. they consist of text and multimedia
   B. the data cannot be stored in a database
   C. they cannot be stored in row and columns
   D. all of the above

9. What would you do to manage corporate unstructured data?
   A. Install big data tool software
   B. Install data integration tools
   C. Install business intelligence software
   D. All of the above

9._____

10. Software-defined data center is a concept for
    A. a virtualized infrastructure
    B. fully automated control of data
    C. hardware maintenance through intelligent software
    D. all of the above

10._____

11. What is a cloud database?
    A. Internet based database provided through cloud data server
    B. Database-as-a-Service
    C. Both A and B
    D. None of the above

11._____

12. Monitor footprint refers to the
    A. disk space of your PC
    B. map of the monitor
    C. space taken up by the monitor on the desk
    D. footprints of the monitor

12._____

13. NOS are already built in
    A. UNIX   B. Mac OS
    C. Windows NT   D. Both A and B

13._____

14. _____ is an example of a network monitoring tool.
    A. Ping   B. VoIP
    C. POP3 server   D. All of the above

14._____

15. Tomato is the name of a wireless router
    A. firmware   B. WRT54GS
    C. both A and B   D. none of the above

15._____

16. _____ is a combination of software and hardware.
    A. Firmware   B. PROM
    C. EPROMs   D. All of the above

16._____

17. Object-oriented fonts are also called
    A. scalable fonts   B. vector fonts
    C. both A and B   D. screen fonts

17._____

18. What is the issue if the computer is rebooting itself?
    A. Faulty power supply   B. Faulty cooling fan
    C. Dirt on the cooling fan D. All of the above

18._____

19. What is the meaning if you receive a message "system running low on virtual memory"?
    A. The system is low on RAM
    B. The hard disc is full
    C. Both A and B
    D. None of the above

20. Your computer freezes on startup. What is the issue?
    A. Defective hardware
    B. Faulty software
    C. Bugged OS
    D. All of the above

21. The computer software maintenance checklist consists of
    A. update virus or install antivirus
    B. delete temporary internet file
    C. clear internet cache
    D. all of the above

22. A CRC error is caused by
    A. a scratched DVD on disk
    B. dirt on CD/DVD
    C. partially burned CDs
    D. all of the above

23. An error message "an invalid Windows File" means
    A. incomplete download
    B. system crash
    C. software bug
    D. all of the above

24. What would you do if it is taking longer than usual to copy files in Windows?
    A. Install an external file such as TeraCopy
    B. Resume broken files
    C. Increase RAM
    D. Both A and B

25. _____ software will help you protect file and folders.
    A. HideFolder
    B. Truecrypt
    C. TeraCopy
    D. None of the above

KEY (CORRECT ANSWERS)

1.	D	11.	C
2.	C	12.	C
3.	C	13.	D
4.	A	14.	D
5.	A	15.	A
6.	A	16.	A
7.	A	17.	C
8.	D	18.	D
9.	D	19.	A
10.	D	20.	D

21. D
22. D
23. D
24. A
25. B

EXAMINATION SECTION
TEST 1

DIRECTIONS: Each question or incomplete statement is followed by several suggested answers or completions. Select the one that BEST answers the question or completes the statement. *PRINT THE LETTER OF THE CORRECT ANSWER IN THE SPACE AT THE RIGHT.*

1. Which of the following is the BEST fact-finding technique that is most helpful in collecting quantitative data?
    A. Interviews
    B. Record reviews and comparisons
    C. Questionnaires
    D. Workshops

2. _____ data is a type of data collected from open-ended questions.
    A. Quantitative
    B. Qualitative
    C. Experimental
    D. Non-official

3. Usually a feasibility study is carried out
    A. after completion of final requirement specification
    B. before the start of the project
    C. before the completion of final requirements specifications
    D. at any time

4. In the analysis phase, which diagram is used to present declaration of the goals and objectives of the project.
    A. Data flow diagram
    B. Entity relationship diagram
    C. Flowchart
    D. Documentation

5. In SDLC, _____ is used to ensure that no alternative is ignored during data analysis.
    A. data flow diagram
    B. organizational chart
    C. Gantt chart
    D. decision table

6. Which of the following software is used to measure hardware and software alternatives?
    A. Automated design tools
    B. DFD
    C. Report generators
    D. Project management

7. _____ is responsible to write Software Requirement Specifications Document (SRS).
    A. Project manager
    B. System analyst
    C. Programmer
    D. User

8. An entity which relates to itself in an ERD model is referred to as _____ relationship.
    A. recursive
    B. one-to-many
    C. many-to-many
    D. one-to-one

9. The goal of normalization is
   A. to increase the number of relations
   B. to increase redundancy
   C. independence of any other relation
   D. to get stable data structure

10. CMM stands for
    A. Capability Maturity Model
    B. Configuration Maturity Model
    C. Capacity Building Manager
    D. Company Management Method

11. Data _____ is terminology used for data accuracy and completeness in any database.
    A. constraint   B. redundancy   C. model   D. integrity

12. A candidate key is defined as
    A. a primary key
    B. the primary key selected to be the key of a relation
    C. an attribute or group of attributes that can be a primary key
    D. both A and B

13. The ability of a class to derive the properties from previously defined class is
    A. encapsulation
    B. polymorphism
    C. information hiding
    D. inheritance

14. A queue data structure stores and retrieves items in a _____ manner.
    A. last in, first out
    B. first in, last out
    C. first in, first out
    D. last in, last out

15. The process of writing a program from an algorithm is called
    A. coding   B. decoding   C. encoding   D. encrypting

16. The CORRECT sequence for creating and executing C++ program is:
    A. Compiling-Editing-Saving-Executing-Linking
    B. Editing-Executing-Compiling-Linking
    C. Editing-Saving-Compiling-Linking-Executing
    D. Linking-Executing-Saving-Compiling

17. As an instructor, you have given your class a programming problem. Every student comes up with a different instruction code for the same problem. Suppose one student has a code of 50 lines, while another has a code of 100 instructions for the same problem.
    Which of the following statements is TRUE?
    A. The greater execution time is required for more instructions than that of less instructions.
    B. Execution time of all programs are the same.
    C. The number of instruction codes does not affect the solution.
    D. Compilation time is greater with more numbers of instruction.

18. In programming languages, a counter can be defined as
    A. the final value of a loop
    B. a variable that counts loop iterations
    C. the initial value of a loop
    D. the stop value of loop

19. Which reserve word is used in programming languages to move the control back to the start of the loop body?
    A. Break   B. Go to   C. Continue   D. Switch

20. The FIRST line in switch block contains the
    A. value of first criterion
    B. statement to be executed if the first criteria is true
    C. expression to be evaluated
    D. statement to be executed if none of the criteria is true

21. What is the output of the following code?
    ```
    int main ()
    {
        int a = 19;
        {
            cout << "value of a: "<<a<<endl;
            a = a + 1;
        }while(a<20);
        return 0;
    }
    ```
    A. 19   B. 20   C. 11   D. 100

22. A computer dedicated to screening access to a network from outside the network is known as
    A. hot site   B. cold site   C. firewall   D. vaccine

23. In anticipation of physical destruction, every organization should have a
    A. biometric scheme   B. disaster recovery plan
    C. DES   D. set of active plan

24. Debug is a term denoting
    A. error correction process
    B. writing of instructions in developing a new program
    C. fault detection in equipment
    D. determine useful life

25. A feature of word processing software to link the name and addresses with a standard document is called
    A. mail merge   B. database management
    C. references   D. review/comment

KEY (CORRECT ANSWERS)

1. C
2. B
3. A
4. C
5. D

6. A
7. A
8. A
9. D
10. A

11. D
12. C
13. D
14. C
15. A

16. C
17. A
18. B
19. C
20. B

21. A
22. C
23. B
24. A
25. A

TEST 2

DIRECTIONS: Each question or incomplete statement is followed by several suggested answers or completions. Select the one that BEST answers the question or completes the statement. *PRINT THE LETTER OF THE CORRECT ANSWER IN THE SPACE AT THE RIGHT.*

1. The SDLC is defined as a process consisting of _____ phases. 1._____
   A. two B. four C. three D. five

2. A framework that describes the set of activities performed at each stage of a software development project is 2._____
   A. SDLC
   B. deployment
   C. waterfall model
   D. SDLC model

3. How is noise defined in terms of software development? 3._____
   A. Writing irrelevant statement to the software development in the SRS document
   B. Adding clashing requirements in the SRS document
   C. Writing over-specific requirements
   D. Writing information about employees

4. Basically, a SWOT analysis is said to be a strategic 4._____
   A. analysis B. measure C. goal D. alignment

5. In the system design phase of the SDLC, _____ is not part of the system's design phase. 5._____
   A. design of alternative systems
   B. writing a systems design report
   C. suggestions of alternative solutions
   D. selection of best system

6. In the system development life cycle, which of the following studies is conducted to determine the possible organizational resistance for a new system? _____ feasibility. 6._____
   A. Organizational B. Operational C. Economic D. Employee

7. The _____ model is BEST suited when organization is very keen and motivated to identify the risk on early stages. 7._____
   A. waterfall B. RAD C. spiral D. incremental

8. Scope of problem is defined with a 8._____
   A. critical path method (CPM) chart
   B. project evaluation and review technique (PERT) chart
   C. data flow diagram (DFD)
   D. context diagram

9. _____ is referred to as a method of database distribution in which different portions of the database reside at different nodes in the network.
   A. Splitting B. Partitioning C. Replication D. Dividing

10. As a computer specialist (software), your client needs an information system that must communicate with existing systems. For that purpose, you need to adopt a design method and accurate linking with the existing system. Your designed system will be
    A. database
    B. system interface
    C. help desks
    D. design interface

11. In entity relation, when primary keys are linked with a foreign key, it forms a _____ relationship between the tables that connect them.
    A. many-to-many
    B. one-to-one
    C. parent-child
    D. server-and-client

12. In normalization, a relation is in a third normal form when no _____ attribute is determining another non-key attribute.
    A. dependent
    B. non-key
    C. key
    D. none of the above

13. In library management databases, which terminology is used to refer to a specific record in your database?
    A. Relation B. Instance C. Table D. Column

14. In database, a rule which describes that foreign key value must match with the primary key value in the other relationship is called
    A. referential integrity constraint
    B. key match rule
    C. entity key group rule
    D. foreign/primary match rule

15. The attribute on the left-hand side of the arrow in a functional dependency is known as
    A. candidate key
    B. determinant
    C. foreign key
    D. primary key

16. A report may be based on a
    A. table
    B. query
    C. relations
    D. both A and B

17. A software program which is used to build reports that summarize data from a database is known as
    A. report writer
    B. reporter
    C. report builder
    D. report generator

18. Which one of the following database objects is created FIRST?
    A. Table B. Form C. Report D. Query

19. In data structures, a ____-linked list does not contain a null pointer at the end of the list.
    A. circular   B. doubly   C. null   D. stacked

20. Polymorphism is described as the
    A. process of returning data from functions by reference
    B. specialization of classes through inheritance
    C. use of classes to represent objects
    D. packaging of data defining an object as a private member variable of class

21. In C++, dynamic binding is useful for the functions that are
    A. overridden   B. defined once
    C. undefined   D. bounded

22. In programming language, a function template is required when
    A. implementation details of function are independent of parameter data types
    B. all functions should be function templates
    C. two different functions have different implementation details
    D. two functions have the same type of parameters

23. _____ are used to group classes for ease of use, maintainability and reusability.
    A. Use cases   B. States   C. Objects   D. Packages

24. The description of structure and organization of data in database is contained in
    A. data dictionary   B. data mine
    C. structured query language D. data mapping

25. What is the output of the following programming code?
    ```
    Int p, q, r;
    P=10, q=3, r=2,
    If (p+q)<14&&(r<q-3)
    Cout <<r;
    Else
    Cout << p;
    ```
    A. -2   B. 4   C. 10   D. -4

KEY (CORRECT ANSWERS)

1.	D	11.	C
2.	D	12.	B
3.	A	13.	B
4.	A	14.	A
5.	C	15.	B
6.	B	16.	D
7.	C	17.	B
8.	D	18.	A
9.	C	19.	A
10.	B	20.	B

21. A
22. D
23. C
24. A
25. C

TEST 3

DIRECTIONS: Each question or incomplete statement is followed by several suggested answers or completions. Select the one that BEST answers the question or completes the statement. *PRINT THE LETTER OF THE CORRECT ANSWER IN THE SPACE AT THE RIGHT.*

1. The parallelogram symbol in a flow chart indicates a
   A. process   B. progress   C. condition   D. input/output

2. A feasibility study in SDLC performs
   A. cost/benefit analysis
   B. designing technique analysis
   C. debugging selection
   D. programming language selection

3. Who is responsible for performing the feasibility study?
   A. Organizational managers
   B. Both organizational manager and system analyst
   C. Users of the proposed system
   D. Both perspective user and systems designers

4. A study of employees' working habits, phobias and obsessions during implementation of a new system is called _____ analysis.
   A. personality   B. cultural feasibility
   C. economic feasibility   D. technological feasibility

5. As a computer specialist (software), a(n) _____ model is based on a regression testing technique.
   A. waterfall   B. RAD   C. V   D. iterative

6. The adaptable model which describes features of the proposed system and is implemented before the installation of the actual system is known as
   A. JAD   B. template   C. RAD   D. prototype

7. Milestones in system development life cycle represent
   A. cost of project   B. status of project
   C. user expectation   D. final product of project

8. Scheduling deadlines and milestones can be shown on a
   A. system survey   B. decision table
   C. prototype   D. Gantt chart

9. Suppose your current organization wants to expand its business into different cities. For that purpose, it needs to distribute business applications across multiple locations. For example, computer systems, storing the data center for Web server, database and telecommunication functions. This is an example of
   A. applications architecture planning
   B. technology architecture planning
   C. enterprise resource planning (ERP)
   D. strategic planning

10. All of the following are components of a physical database EXCEPT
    A. file organization
    B. data volume
    C. data distribution
    D. normalize the relations

11. Suppose working as a computer specialist (software) your organization has assigned you a task to develop a database for an academic institution. Which one is the MOST appropriate association in the database for a class that might have multiple prerequisites?
    A. Generalization association
    B. N-ary association
    C. Aggregation association
    D. Reflexive association

12. While working on an academic institute database, according to you, which one is the MOST suitable special association to model a course that has an instructor, teaching assistants, a classroom, meeting time slot and class schedule?
    A. Generalization association
    B. N-ary association
    C. Aggregation association
    D. Reflexive association

13. Which one of the following is the MOST suitable association that shows that multiple textbooks for a course are required to make a reading list?
    A. Aggregation association
    B. Generalization association
    C. N-ary association
    D. Reflexive association

14. In parameters, passing by value
    A. actual parameters and formal parameters must be similar types
    B. actual parameters and formal parameters can be different types
    C. parameters passing by value can be used both for input and output purpose
    D. both A and B

15. In data structures, which of the following can be used to facilitate adding nodes to the end of the linear linked list?
    A. Head pointer
    B. Zero head node
    C. Tail pointer
    D. Precede pointer

16. A full binary tree with n leaves consist of _____ nodes.
    A. n
    B. 2^{n-1}
    C. n-1
    D. log n

17. Linear model and prototyping model are combined to form a _____ model.
    A. waterfall
    B. incremental
    C. build & fix
    D. spiral

18. An example of query is
    A. selection of all records that match a set of criteria
    B. importing spreadsheet file into the database
    C. search for specific record
    D. both A and C are correct

19. The database development process involves mapping of conceptual data model into a(n) _____ model.
    A. object-oriented
    B. network data
    C. implementation
    D. hierarchical data

20. In database, one field or combination of fields for which more than one record may have the same combination of values is called the
    A. secondary key
    B. index
    C. composite key
    D. linked key

21. Customers, cars and parts are examples of
    A. entities
    B. attributes
    C. cardinals
    D. relationships

22. A ping program used to send a multiple packet to a server to check its ability to handle a quantity of traffic maliciously is called
    A. pagejacking
    B. jam sync
    C. ping storm
    D. ping strangeness

23. Which one of the following is the key factor to develop a new system to manage a disaster?
    A. Equipment replacement
    B. Unfavorable weather
    C. Lack of insurance coverage
    D. Loss of processing ability

24. As a computer specialist (software), you ask 100 client organization employees to fill out a survey that includes questions about educational background, their job type, salary and amount spent on purchases of a widget annually. After you enter the data in a spreadsheet program, you decide to look for a relationship between income and the amount spent on widgets. The BEST way to display the data for this kind of assumption is a _____ chart.
    A. bullet
    B. line
    C. pic
    D. scatter

25. Suppose it is your very first day of your job. When you turn on your computer, the system unit is visibly on but the monitor is dark. What is the exact issue?
    A. The monitor model is too old to work
    B. The operating system is not working
    C. The monitor is not connected to the PC
    D. Call the help desk officer

KEY (CORRECT ANSWERS)

1.	D		11.	D
2.	A		12.	B
3.	A		13.	C
4.	B		14.	A
5.	D		15.	C
6.	D		16.	B
7.	B		17.	B
8.	D		18.	D
9.	B		19.	C
10.	D		20.	A

21. A
22. C
23. D
24. D
25. C

TEST 4

DIRECTIONS: Each question or incomplete statement is followed by several suggested answers or completions. Select the one that BEST answers the question or completes the statement. *PRINT THE LETTER OF THE CORRECT ANSWER IN THE SPACE AT THE RIGHT.*

1. A collection of logically related data elements that can be used for multiple processing needs is called
    A. files
    B. a register
    C. a database
    D. organization

    1.____

2. For the purpose of data gathering, your organization and client have secretly engaged you in the client group that is being studied. You are considered a(n)
    A. observer-as-participant
    B. observer
    C. complete participant
    D. part-time employee

    2.____

3. For data gathering, interviews in which the topics are pre-decided but the sequence and phrasing can be adapted during the interview is called a(n)
    A. informal conversational interview
    B. closed quantitative interview
    C. standardized open-ended interview
    D. interview-guided approach

    3.____

4. In SDLC, which of the following analysis methods is adopted to start with the "intricate image" and then breaks it down into smaller sections?
    A. Financial
    B. Bottom up
    C. Reverse
    D. Top-down
    E. Executive

    4.____

5. As a computer specialist (software), which one of the following is the biggest reason for the failure of system development projects?
    A. Lack of JAD sessions
    B. Purchasing COTS
    C. Imprecise or missing business requirements
    D. Hurdles from employees

    5.____

6. The _____ model is the BEST suited model to create client/server applications.
    A. waterfall
    B. spiral
    C. incremental
    D. concurrent

    6.____

7. Which hardware component is essential for function of a database management system?
    A. Larger capacity, high speed disk
    B. Mouse
    C. High resolution monitors
    D. Printer

    7.____

8. _____ refers to a method of database distribution in which one database contains data that are included in another database.
    A. Splitting
    B. Partitioning
    C. Replication
    D. Dividing

    8.____

9. In the database design process, which one of the following is referred to modality?
   A. Optional
   B. Mandatory
   C. Unidirectional
   D. Both A and B

10. According to the research conducted by an international professional organization, out of 100 most occupied jobs that they researched, the top job classification was a
    A. database administrator
    B. cryptographer
    C. programmer
    D. computer engineer

11. In the database, different attributes in two different tables having the same name are referred to as
    A. a synonym
    B. a homonym
    C. an acronym
    D. mutually exclusive

12. Consider two tables: Class and Student are related by a "one-to-many relationship. In which table should the corresponding foreign key be placed?
    A. Only Class table requires foreign key.
    B. Only Student table requires foreign key.
    C. Both tables require foreign key.
    D. Composite entity must be added so foreign keys will be required in both Class and Student tables.

13. [E-R diagram: Table A —1— ◇ —M— Table B]

    Using the above E-R diagram, which one of the following statements is TRUE?
    A. Both tables should have the same number of (primary) key attributes.
    B. Table A should have a larger number of key attributes.
    C. Table B should have a larger number of key attributes.
    D. The diagram does not propose which table might have more attributes in its primary key.

14. Which form of functional dependency is the set of attributes that is neither a subset or any of the keys nor the candidate key?
    A. Full functional dependency
    B. Partial dependency
    C. Primary functional dependency
    D. Transitive dependency

15. The true dependencies are formed by the _____ rule.
    A. reflexive
    B. referential
    C. inferential
    D. termination

16. Which facility helps DBMS to synchronize its files and journals while occasionally suspending all processing?
    A. Checkpoint facility
    B. Backup recovery
    C. Recovery manager
    D. Database change log

17. In data structures, which one of the following operations is used to retrieve and then remove the top of the stack?
    A. Create Stack
    B. Push
    C. Pop
    D. Pull

18. Class definition
    A. must have a constructor specified
    B. must end with a semicolon
    C. provides the class interface
    D. both B and C

19. Which operator is used in compound condition to join two conditions?
    A. Relational operator
    B. Logical operator
    C. Relational result
    D. Logical result

20. The conditional portion of IF statements can contain any
    A. valid expression
    B. expression that can be evaluated to Boolean value
    C. valid variable
    D. valid constant or variable

21. System analysts suggest that telecommuting will become more popular with managers and client teams when
    A. workers are forced to telecommute
    B. the manager finally gives up the idea of controlling the worker
    C. multimedia teleconferencing system becomes affordable
    D. automobiles become outdated

22. Error reports are an example of _____ reports.
    A. scheduled
    B. exception
    C. on-demand
    D. external

23. Word processing, electronic filling, and electronic mails are part of
    A. help desk
    B. electronic industry
    C. office automation
    D. official tasks

24. In a word processor, the block that appears at the top and bottom of every page which display deals is called the
    A. top and bottom margin
    B. headline and end note
    C. title and page number
    D. header and footer

25. In word processing software, _____ are inserted as a cross-reference.
    A. placeholders
    B. bookmarks
    C. objects
    D. word fields

KEY (CORRECT ANSWERS)

1. C
2. C
3. D
4. B
5. C

6. D
7. A
8. C
9. D
10. D

11. C
12. B
13. D
14. D
15. A

16. A
17. C
18. A
19. D
20. A

21. C
22. B
23. C
24. D
25. D

EXAMINATION SECTION
TEST 1

DIRECTIONS: Each question or incomplete statement is followed by several suggested answers or completions. Select the one that BEST answers the question or completes the statement. *PRINT THE LETTER OF THE CORRECT ANSWER IN THE SPACE AT THE RIGHT.*

1. What is VGA?
   A. Video Graphics Array
   B. Video Graphics Adapter
   C. Visual Graphics Array
   D. None of the above

2. IBM 1401 was a
   A. fourth generation computer
   B. second generation computer
   C. third generation computer
   D. none of the above

3. A micro program is a collection of
   A. large scale operations
   B. DMA
   C. registers
   D. microinstructions

4. The time a CPU takes to recognize an interrupt request is called
   A. interrupt latency
   B. timer delay
   B. response deadline
   D. throughput

5. A _____ regulates the arrangement of the flow of microinstructions.
   A. multiplexer
   B. micro program controller
   C. DMA controller
   D. virtual memory

6. Which of the following techniques will not be used when CPU exchanges data with a peripheral device?
   A. Interrupt driven I/O
   B. Direct Memory Access (DMA)
   C. Programmed I/O
   D. Virtual memory

7. If a prior received character is not read by CPU and overwritten by new character received, the error will be called a _____ error.
   A. framing   B. parity   C. overrun   D. under-run

8. Which of the following networks needs manual routing?
   A. Fiber optic   B. Bus   C. T-switched   D. Ring

9. Which layer of TCP/IP responds to the OSI models to three layers?
   A. Application   B. Presentation   C. Session   D. Transport

10. _____ transport layer protocols is connectionless.
    A. UDP   B. TCP   C. FTP   D. NVT

43

11. _____ applications permit a user to approach and modify/change remote files without physical transfer.
    A. DNS B. FTP C. NFS D. Telnet

12. Which of the following is a non-impact and quiet printer?
    A. Inkjet B. Laser C. Thermal D. Dot matrix

13. Which of the following are high-end printers?
    A. Inkjet B. Laser C. Thermal D. Dot matrix

14. For the purpose of plotting designs and graphs on papers, _____ is/are used.
    A. trackball B. joystick C. light pen D. plotters

15. What is a Snowbol?
    A. Operating system B. HLL
    C. Software D. Search engine

16. Which of the following connects to a modem?
    A. Telephone line B. Keyboard C. Printer D. Monitor

17. In automated organizations, _____ processing is used by large transaction processing systems.
    A. online B. batch C. once-a-day D. end-of-day

18. What should a technician do after addition of a new cable segment to the network?
    A. Revise the disaster recovery plan
    B. Update the changes in document
    C. Update the wiring schematics
    D. None of the above

19. For the purpose of breaking up a broadcast domain, a _____ can be used.
    A. bridge B. router
    C. DHCP server D. printer

20. The secure way of transferring files between two devices is
    A. SFTP B. SNMPv3 C. TFTP D. FTP

21. An administrator networking closet (with all the networking and communication equipment) is on the second floor of a building and the communications lines are installed on the first floor. A _____ will be extended to connect communication lines to the networking closet.
    A. smart jack B. demarcation point
    C. patch panel D. router

22. To provide access to a VPN, _____ is used.
    A. IGP B. PPTP C. PPP D. RAS

23. Two users are directly linked via RJ-45 and CAT5e cables and are communicating through IP. If the first user transmits data out of the RJ-45 on pins 1 and 2, the client should expect to receive a response on pins
    A. 1 and 2   B. 2 and 4   C. 3 and 6   D. 4 and 6

24. Examination of physical hardware addresses is done in _____ network access security method.
    A. IP filtering   B. L2TP   C. MAC filtering   D. RAS

25. Wireless standards give the direct advantage of
    A. increased use of wireless spectrum
    B. greater device security
    C. interoperability between devices
    D. increased number of protocols can be used

KEY (CORRECT ANSWERS)

1.	A	11.	C
2.	B	12.	A
3.	D	13.	B
4.	A	14.	D
5.	B	15.	D
6.	D	16.	A
7.	C	17.	B
8.	C	18.	C
9.	A	19.	B
10.	A	20.	A

21. C
22. B
23. C
24. C
25. C

TEST 2

DIRECTIONS: Each question or incomplete statement is followed by several suggested answers or completions. Select the one that BEST answers the question or completes the statement. *PRINT THE LETTER OF THE CORRECT ANSWER IN THE SPACE AT THE RIGHT.*

1. What is an ALU? 1.____
   A. Arithmetic Logic Unit
   B. Array Logic Unit
   C. Application Logic Unit
   D. None of the above

2. In a client-server system, which type of computers are usually client computers? 2.____
   A. Mainframe
   B. Mini computer
   C. Micro computer
   D. PDA

3. A(n) _____ is necessary for a computer to *boot*. 3.____
   A. compiler
   B. loader
   C. operating system
   D. assembler

4. In the present technology age, computers are typically 4.____
   A. digital   B. analog   C. hybrid   D. complex

5. What is the physical structure of a computer called? 5.____
   A. CPU   B. Hardware   C. Software   D. All of the above

6. Data is represented in the form of discrete signals in a(n) _____ computer. 6.____
   A. analog   B. digital   C. both A and B   D. hybrid

7. _____ is now available in the form of PC. 7.____
   A. Mainframe
   B. Micro computer
   C. Mini computer
   D. Both B and C

8. Which of the following is larger than a portable computer but is a small general function micro computer? 8.____
   A. Hybrid
   B. Digital
   C. Desktop
   D. None of the above

9. Most of the processing in a computer takes place in 9.____
   A. memory   B. RAM   C. both A and B   D. CPU

10. What does LAN stand for? 10.____
    A. Limited Area Network
    B. Logical Area Network
    C. Local Area Network
    D. Large Area Network

11. Which of the following defines the rules and procedures for regulating data transmission over the internet? 11.____
    A. IP address   B. Domains   C. Protocol   D. Gateway

12. Which of the following protocol is used by the intranets, extranets and internet? 12.____
    A. TCP/IP   B. Protocol
    C. Open system   D. Internet work processor

13. On which ring does the data travel in FDDI? 13.____
    A. The primary   B. The secondary
    C. Both rings   D. None of the above

14. _____ is the logical topology. 14.____
    A. Bus   B. Tree   C. Star   D. Both A and C

15. The main drawback of ring topology is that 15.____
    A. if one computer fails, it affects the whole network
    B. adding/removing computers affects the network activity
    C. failure of the central hub makes the whole network unable to work
    D. both A and B

16. _____ is NOT anti-virus software. 16.____
    A. NAV   B. F-Prot   C. Oracle   D. McAfee

17. DMA stands for 17.____
    A. Direct Memory Allocation   B. Direct Memory Access
    C. Direct Module Access   D. none of the above

18. Which of the following is a storage device? 18.____
    A. Tape   B. Hard disk
    C. Floppy disk   D. All of the above

19. Which of the following are determined by user needs? 19.____
    A. System software   B. Application software
    C. Assemblers   D. Compilers

20. Which tools are available with system analysis? 20.____
    A. Review of procedure and conducting interviews
    B. Review of documentation and observation of the situation
    C. Conducting interviews and questionnaire administration
    D. Both B and C

21. Programs used to catch errors and their causes are called 21.____
    A. operating system extensions   B. cookies
    C. diagnostic software   D. boot diskettes

22. A virus which reproduces itself by using the computer host is called 22.____
    A. time bomb   B. worm
    C. Melissa virus   D. macro virus

23. The best practice for implementing a basic wireless network is   23._____
    A. disabling ESSID broadcast
    B. adding two access points per area of service
    C. not configuring the ESSID point
    D. none of the above

24. For connecting a single network node to a switch, _____ wiring standards   24._____
    will usually be used.
    A. loopback   B. straight   C. rollover   D. crossover

25. Before having a db loss, a CAT5 cable can run a maximum distance of   25._____
    A. 106 feet (31 meters)   B. 203 feet (60 meters)
    C. 328 feet (100 meters)   D. none of the above

KEY (CORRECT ANSWERS)

1.	A		11.	C
2.	C		12.	A
3.	C		13.	A
4.	A		14.	C
5.	B		15.	D
6.	B		16.	C
7.	B		17.	B
8.	C		18.	D
9.	D		19.	A
10.	C		20.	D

21.	C
22.	B
23.	A
24.	B
25.	C

TEST 3

DIRECTIONS: Each question or incomplete statement is followed by several suggested answers or completions. Select the one that BEST answers the question or completes the statement. *PRINT THE LETTER OF THE CORRECT ANSWER IN THE SPACE AT THE RIGHT.*

1. I/O port is an interface that is used to connect microcomputer bus to
    A. flip flops
    B. memory
    C. peripheral devices
    D. multiplexers

2. In _____, a CPU poll after detecting an interrupt, determines the interrupting module and branches in an interrupt service routine.
    A. daisy chain
    B. software poll
    C. multiple interrupts lines
    D. all of the above

3. Where is a separate address space for an I/O operation reserved for a CPU?
    A. Isolated I/O
    B. Memory mapped I/O
    C. Memory
    D. None of the above

4. In _____ for resolving the priority, the highest priority device is placed at the first position followed by less priority devices.
    A. asynchronous methods
    B. daisy-chaining priority methods
    C. parallel method
    D. semi-synchronous method

5. In _____, a part of the CPU's address lines constructing an input to the address decoder is neglected.
    A. microprogramming
    B. instruction pre-fetching
    C. pipelining
    D. partial decoding

6. What is the data unit in TCP/IP called?
    A. Message   B. Segment   C. Datagram   D. Frame

7. If a host domain name is known, what can DNS obtain?
    A. Station address
    B. IP address
    C. Port address
    D. Checksum

8. _____ OSI layers correspond to TCP/IP's application layer.
    A. Application
    B. Presentation
    C. Session
    D. All of the above

9. Devices on different networks can communicate with each other via a
    A. file server
    B. gateway
    C. printer server
    D. none of the above

10. Which of the following can combine transmissions from different input/output devices into one line?
    A. Concentrator communication device
    B. Modifier
    C. Multiplexer
    D. Full duplex line

11. For the analysis of retinal scans, fingerprints, etc. in security access systems, which of the following techniques is used?
    A. Biometrics
    B. Bio measurement
    C. Computer security
    D. Smart weapon machinery

12. _____ guards a computer against unauthorized access to a network.
    A. Hacker-proof antivirus
    B. Firewall
    C. Encryption safe wall
    D. All of the above

13. What is scrambling of code called?
    A. Encryption
    B. Firewall
    C. Scrambling
    D. Password proofing

14. What should be used to prevent data loss due to power failure?
    A. Encryption program
    B. Surge protector
    C. Firewall
    D. UPS

15. If an administrator wants to install a device which can detect and control peer-to-peer traffic, a _____ device type will be installed.
    A. bandwidth shaper
    B. intrusion detection
    C. proxy server
    D. load balancer

16. If a technician needs to troubleshoot an unfamiliar network, the first step taken to diagnose the problem would be to
    A. report the problem to administrative technician
    B. make use of a port analyzer to analyze the network topology
    C. analyze symptoms and draw a network diagram
    D. all of the above

17. To discover MAC address of a connecting router, _____ commands can be used.
    A. ARP B. trace route C. ping D. ping sweep

18. E-mails sent to users with malicious website links are an example of
    A. viruses
    B. phishing
    C. rogue access points
    D. man-in-the-middle

19. To analyze that a RJ-45 jack in a cubicle responds to a specific RJ-45 jack in a patch panel, an administrator will use a
    A. punch-down tool
    B. spectrum analyzer
    C. toner probe
    D. multi-meter

20. _____ network types are suitable for a 10 gigabyte core network using 33 feet (10 meter) fiber runs.
    A. 10Base-FX
    B. 10GBase-SR
    C. 10GBase-SW
    D. None of the above

21. When an administrator troubleshoots network connectivity and wants to view which packets are going through from workstation X to server 1, he will use _____ command line tools.
    A. view route
    B. route
    C. trace route
    D. ping

22. For the purpose of updating physical network diagrams, revising _____ is the most appropriate policy.
    A. whenever a connection is changed
    B. before regularly scheduled network audits
    C. after new personnel are hired
    D. after weekly network support team review

23. When a firewall accepts a request packet on port 80, it allows the reply packet to pass through automatically. This behavior of firewall is best described as
    A. stateful inspection
    B. intrusion detection
    C. content filtering
    D. passive fingerprinting

24. A network technician can face _____ connectivity issues as a result of bundling network cables tightly together.
    A. collision
    B. attenuation
    C. crosstalk
    D. open circuit

25. On a wireless network, a _____ mechanism uses a separate network authentication server.
    A. Kerberos
    B. TKIP
    C. RADIUS
    D. WEP

KEY (CORRECT ANSWERS)

1.	C		11.	A
2.	B		12.	B
3.	A		13.	A
4.	C		14.	D
5.	D		15.	A
6.	D		16.	C
7.	B		17.	A
8.	D		18.	B
9.	B		19.	D
10.	C		20.	B

21. C
22. A
23. A
24. C
25. C

TEST 4

DIRECTIONS: Each question or incomplete statement is followed by several suggested answers or completions. Select the one that BEST answers the question or completes the statement. *PRINT THE LETTER OF THE CORRECT ANSWER IN THE SPACE AT THE RIGHT.*

1. The electrical pathway through which the processor communicates with peripheral devices is called the
   A. computer bus   B. hazard   C. memory   D. disk

   1.____

2. If a 0 is transmitted instead of a stop bit, a(n) _____ error will be the serial communication error condition.
   A. framing   B. parity   C. overrun   D. under-run

   2.____

3. An interrupt can be defined as a process where
   A. an external device can speed up the working of the microprocessor
   B. input devices can take over the working of the microprocessor
   C. an external device gets the attention of the microprocessor
   D. none of the above

   3.____

4. What controls the sequence of the flow of microinstructions?
   A. Multiplexer   B. Micro program controller
   C. DMA controller   D. Virtual memory

   4.____

5. What is MSI?
   A. Medium Scale Integrated Circuits
   B. Medium System Intelligence
   C. Medium Scale Intelligent Circuit
   D. None of the above

   5.____

6. If a network has N number of devices and every device has N-1 ports for cables, this topology is known as
   A. mesh   B. star   C. bus   D. ring

   6.____

7. Usenet is also known as
   A. Gopher   B. Newsgroups   C. Browser   D. CERN

   7.____

8. Junk e-mail is also known as
   A. spam   B. spoof   C. sniffer script   D. spool

   8.____

9. Geographical scattered office LANS can be connected by
   A. VAN   B. LAN   C. DAN   D. WAN

   9.____

10. _____ gathers information of the user and sends it to someone over the internet.
    A. A virus   B. Spybot
    C. Logic bomb   D. Security patch

    10.____

53

2 (#4)

11. A worm virus is terminated eventually due to the lack of
    A. memory or disk space   B. time
    C. CD drive space   D. CD-RW

12. Instructions of a computer are executed by direct involvement of the
    A. scanner   B. main storage
    C. secondary storage   D. processor

13. Most processing of a computer takes place in
    A. memory   B. RAM   C. motherboard   D. CPU

14. Which of the following is NOT a storage medium?
    A. Hard disk   B. Flash drive   C. DVD   D. Scanner

15. Suppose a user calls you for network support and says that his e-mail is not working. What will you do first?
    A. Inquire about the operation performed by the user and what was the expected and actual result
    B. Restart the hub the user was connected to
    C. Send a test e-mail message to see if it's sent
    D. None of the above

16. Suppose two networks in different departments are using DHCP set up for 192.168.0.0/24 and after consolidation of the officer's network we have run out of IP addresses. The BEST cost-effective solution for this will be
    A. adding a router to connect both networks
    B. switching to static IP addressing
    C. changing the subnet mask to 255.255.254.0
    D. none of the above

17. Suppose that packets to an IP address are getting lost over the internet. Which tools will an administrator use to find out the responsible hop?
    A. Ping   B. nslookup   C. Trace route   D. netstat

18. What should a technician check if a workstation on the network is able to ping hosts on the network but it is not able to ping any addresses on the internet?
    A. The DNS server entries   B. The network card
    C. The default gateway   D. The host's file

19. To find out the status of all established TCP connections by port 80, the administrator will use the _____ command.
    A. netstat –at   B. netstat –r   C. netstat –v   D. netstat -p tcp

20. To evaluate the network traffic, which of the following tools will be used?
    A. OTDR   B. Protocol analyzer
    C. Certifier   D. Toner probe

21. Which port is usually used for FTP traffic? 21.____
    A. 20   B. 22   C. 23   D. 25

22. _____ can function as a router, support VLANs and connect multiple workstations. 22.____
    A. Repeater   B. Switch
    C. Hub   D. Multilayer switch

23. 208.177.23.1 belongs to class 23.____
    A. A   B. B   C. C   D. D

24. If 25 clients on the same network want to see a video, _____ should be configured on the user's computer to reduce network traffic. 24.____
    A. class C addresses   B. class A addresses
    C. broadcast   D. multicast

25. Suppose we have installed a new LAN switch on fiber ports. In order to allow compatibility to the existing fiber network, what will a technician need on the new switch? 25.____
    A. Router   B. Repeater
    C. Media converter   D. Hub

KEY (CORRECT ANSWERS)

1.	A		11.	A
2.	A		12.	D
3.	C		13.	D
4.	B		14.	D
5.	A		15.	A
6.	A		16.	C
7.	B		17.	C
8.	A		18.	C
9.	D		19.	D
10.	B		20.	B

21. A
22. D
23. C
24. D
25. C

EXAMINATION SECTION
TEST 1

DIRECTIONS: Each question or incomplete statement is followed by several suggested answers or completions. Select the one that BEST answers the question or completes the statement. *PRINT THE LETTER OF THE CORRECT ANSWER IN THE SPACE AT THE RIGHT.*

1. Modern day telephony uses _____ for sending voice signals.   1._____
   A. VoIP   B. modems   C. routers   D. switches

2. A user is downloading a file using a computer on the network. The computer is a(n)   2._____
   A. node   B. entry point   C. client   D. access point

3. A network operating system offers its services to   3._____
   A. groups of computers using desktop operating system
   B. groups of servers connected to LAN
   C. users in another network segment
   D. all of the above

4. The program to interpret HTML files sent from a web server is called   4._____
   A. browser
   B. SMTP server
   C. RAS
   D. HTML engine

5. FrameRelay is used in   5._____
   A. LAN   B. MAN   C. WAN   D. PAN

6. The most secure network is   6._____
   A. LAN   B. MAN   C. WAN   D. PAN

7. In a _____ network, any computer could be a client or server.   7._____
   A. peer-to-peer
   B. client server
   B. VLAN
   D. terrestrial

8. User documents have been stored on a central server for printing. This is an example of a(n) _____ server.   8._____
   A. application   B. file   C. print   D. mail

9. Small computer programs are being run from a central computer. This is a(n) _____ kind of server.   9._____
   A. application   B. file   c. print   D. mail

10. Databases are stored in a(n) _____ server.   10._____
    A. database   B. file   C. data   D. information

11. Data resources are placed at different geographical locations, however, they are managed from one unique location. What kind of network model is this?   11._____
    A. Centralized   B. Remote   C. Distributed   D. Isolated

12. A company has a private network used within its premises. It has given access to a few outside suppliers through its
    A. intranet   B. extranet   C. internet   D. subnet   12.____

13. You are using your browser to browse a web page using HTTP protocol. _____ protocol will be used to respond to your request.
    A. HTTP   B. TCP   C. HTTPS   D. IP   13.____

14. _____ protocols are not specific to one supplier of LAN equipment.
    A. Proprietary   B. Functional   C. Universal   D. Standard   14.____

15. RFCs are used to upgrade the bandwidth requirements of a protocol. RFC stands for
    A. Requirement for Formal Consent   B. Regional Formats Committee
    C. Request For Comments   D. Released Future Concerns   15.____

16. LAN standards for networking are developed by _____ organization.
    A. IERT   B. IEEE   C. FERS   D. OOEE   16.____

17. Standard allocation of Internet protocol addresses are insured by an organization called
    A. ICANN   B. Internet Architecture Board (IAB)
    C. IEEE   D. Internet Society   17.____

18. A network switch is connected to 15 employees. _____ topology is in use.
    A. Star   B. Bus   C. Ring   D. Hybrid   18.____

19. _____ optic fiber cable will be used for smaller distances.
    A. Single Mode Fiber (SMF)   B. Multi-Mode Fiber (MMF)
    C. Both A and B   D. None of the above   19.____

20. The entire bandwidth of a digital signal is being used by the only channel. It is called a(n) _____ communication.
    A. broadband   B. digital   C. analog   D. baseband   20.____

21. Frequency Division Multiplexing (FDM) is possible in
    A. baseband   B. broadband
    C. both A and B   D. none of the above   21.____

22. Gigabit Ethernet is capable of transmissions of 1000
    A. BPS   B. GBPS   C. MBPS   D. KBPS   22.____

23. Fiber distributed data interface uses _____ topology.
    A. ring   B. star   C. mesh   D. bus   23.____

24. IEEE networking standards apply to the _____ layer specifications technology.
    A. network   B. data   C. application   D. physical   24.____

25. Mutual authentication between the client and the server is called 25.____
 A. encrypted B. decrypted
 C. challenge handshake D. kerberos

KEY (CORRECT ANSWERS)

1.	A	11.	C
2.	C	12.	B
3.	D	13.	A
4.	A	14.	D
5.	C	15.	C
6.	A	16.	B
7.	A	17.	A
8.	B	18.	A
9.	A	19.	A
10.	A	20.	D

21. B
22. C
23. A
24. A
25. A

TEST 2

DIRECTIONS: Each question or incomplete statement is followed by several suggested answers or completions. Select the one that BEST answers the question or completes the statement. *PRINT THE LETTER OF THE CORRECT ANSWER IN THE SPACE AT THE RIGHT.*

1. Fast Ethernet can run on
   A. UTP
   B. optical fiber
   C. wireless
   D. all of the above

2. Fiber fast Ethernet can provide speeds of up to
   A. 1 GBPS   B. 512 MBPS   C. 100 MBPS   D. 256 KBPS

3. Giga-Ethernet provides speed up to _____ MBPS over fiber.
   A. 1000   B. 512   C. 256   D. 1.5

4. _____ LAN is a solution to divide a single broadcast domain into multiple broadcast domains.
   A. Virtual   B. Localized   C. Bridged   D. Broadcast

5. Internet uses _____ topology.
   A. hybrid   B. daisy chain   C. dual ring   D. mesh

6. Unlike OSI, the Internet model uses _____ layers.
   A. 3   B. 4   C. 7   D. 5

7. Infrared frequency ranges from 300 GHz to 43 THz and is used for
   A. TV remotes
   B. penetrating obstacles
   C. communications of up to 1000 meters
   D. line of sight communication

8. Frequency Division Multiplexing (FDM) uses _____ to distribute bandwidth.
   A. frequency   B. channels   C. time slots   D. path

9. _____ is used to provide abstraction of services.
   A. Abstraction layer
   B. Network layer
   C. Encapsulation
   D. Collision detection

10. _____ are addressed via ports.
   A. Processes
   B. Memory address
   C. NIC
   D. Protocols

2 (#2)

11. SMTP is _____-level protocol. 11.____
    A. higher   B. lower   C. user   D. network

12. _____ layer provides host-to-host communications. 12.____
    A. Network   B. Data   C. Transport   D. Physical

13. _____ is basic transport layer protocol. 13.____
    A. UDP   B. HTTP   C. HTTPS   D. FTP

14. Adding a packet header is a function of 14.____
    A. transport   B. physical   C. data link   D. application

15. _____ requires sending from one network to another. 15.____
    A. Internetworking   B. Transmission control
    C. TCP   D. IP

16. A host is identified using 16.____
    A. IP addressing system   B. website address
    C. MAC address   D. Checksum

17. 128-bit addressing is made possible by 17.____
    A. IPV4   B. IPV6   C. TCP/IP   D. UDP

18. HDLC stands for 18.____
    A. High Level Link Control   B. High Level Data Level Checking
    C. High Definition Latency Check   D. High Definition Least Control

19. IP (Internet Protocol) does NOT guarantee _____ delivery. 19.____
    A. reliable   B. efficient   C. error-free   D. complete

20. Routers and _____ do not examine traffic. 20.____
    A. graphic cards   B. bridges
    C. network hubs   d switches

21. A PAN may use _____ protocol. 21.____
    A. Bluetooth   B. IP   C. TCP   D. UDP

22. A wireless router typically allows devices to connect to 22.____
    A. a wired network
    B. a wireless network
    C. both wired and wireless networks
    D. predefined devices on other networks

23. _____ may refer to a Wi-Fi use without permission. 23.____
    A. Piggybacking   B. Address breach
    C. Access point hack   D. IP address violation

24. FTTN in fiber networks denotes Fiber
    A. Technology Tracking Network
    B. to the Neighborhood
    C. Transmission Twisted Network
    D. Traceability Track Nationwide

25. PON stands for _____ Network.
    A. Passive Optic
    B. Private Optic
    C. Privately Owned
    D. Primary Operational

KEY (CORRECT ANSWERS)

1.	D		11.	A
2.	C		12.	C
3.	A		13.	A
4.	A		14.	C
5.	A		15.	A
6.	B		16.	A
7.	A		17.	B
8.	B		18.	A
9.	C		19.	A
10.	A		20.	D

21. A
22. C
23. A
24. B
25. A

TEST 3

DIRECTIONS: Each question or incomplete statement is followed by several suggested answers or completions. Select the one that BEST answers the question or completes the statement. *PRINT THE LETTER OF THE CORRECT ANSWER IN THE SPACE AT THE RIGHT.*

1. MIMO stands for
   A. Multiple Input Multiple Output
   B. Multiple Inter Modular Operations
   C. Metropolitan Inter Module Onset
   D. Metropolitan Intra Modular Offnet

2. Beamforming characterizes
   A. merging of optic fiber streams
   B. merging of signals
   C. line of sight light beams
   D. unidirectional radio streams

3. Speed of transmission will be SLOWEST in
   A. LAN   B. WAN   C. MAN   D. PAN

4. Network Interface Cards (NIC) use a(n) _____ to distinguish one computer from another.
   A. network address
   B. IP address
   C. MAC address
   D. Checksum

5. Which of the following amplify communication signals and filter noise?
   A. Hubs   B. Switches   C. Routers   D. Repeaters

6. _____ send information/data to be copied unmodified to all computers.
   A. Hubs   B. Bridges   C. Firewalls   D. Switches

7. Which of the following reject network access requests from unsafe sources?
   A. Filter services
   B. Hubs
   C. Security protocols
   D. Firewalls

8. A _____ normally represents the smallest amount of data that can traverse over a network at a single time.
   A. byte   B. bit   C. word   D. packet

9. OSPF is a
   A. routing protocol
   B. unique addressing scheme
   C. end user identification technique
   D. open source software

10. _____ route is used when failure occurs with a routing device.
    A. Adaptive   B. Alternate   C. Access   D. Appropriate

11. _____ is a parameter used for calculating a routing metric.
    A. Path speed   B. Load   C. Hop count   D. All of the above

12. Algorithm in computer operations is a
    A. software   B. hardware   C. method   D. pseudo code

13. _____ is the total time a packet takes to transmit from one place to another.
    A. Response time   B. Latency
    C. Delay   D. Bandwidth

14. Media portion in an OSI model includes
    A. presentation and data layer
    B. application and network layer
    C. transport and data layer
    D. all of the network data link and physical layers

15. OSI stands for Open
    A. Systems Interconnection   B. Standards International
    C. Systems Integration   D. Standards for Internet

16. Collision occurs when
    A. packets collide due to throttling
    B. more than one computer sends data at the same time
    C. data is sent out of sequence
    D. network traffic exceeds its limit

17. CSMA is a method used by
    A. Ethernet   B. Internet
    C. operating system   D. error detection services

18. The term broadband is used when a media type
    A. can carry multiple data signals
    B. can carry one signal at one time
    C. has separate lines for sending and receiving
    D. has error detection and correction mechanism

19. Fast Ethernet is also known as
    A. 10 Base-T   B. 100 Base-T
    C. Gigabit Ethernet   D. 1000 Base-X

20. _____ is called beacon frame.
    A. Periodically broadcasted frame   B. Identification frame
    C. Header frame   D. Frame beginning the broadcast

21. Channel bonding allows multiple _____ at the same time.
    A. packets   B. channels   C. media   D. data streams

22. Gigabit Ethernet works on _____ media.
    A. fiber optic   B. copper
    C. both fiber and copper   D. wireless

23. FDDI uses _____ rings. 23.____
    A. four B. two C. one D. three

24. IPV6 addresses are _____ bits. 24.____
    A. 32 B. 65 C. 128 D. 256

25. IPV6 addresses are binary numbers represented in 25.____
    A. decimal B. binary C. octal D. hexadecimal

KEY (CORRECT ANSWERS)

1.	A	11.	D
2.	D	12.	C
3.	C	13.	B
4.	C	14.	D
5.	D	15.	A
6.	A	16.	B
7.	D	17.	A
8.	D	18.	A
9.	A	19.	B
10.	A	20.	A

21. B
22. C
23. B
24. C
25. D

TEST 4

DIRECTIONS: Each question or incomplete statement is followed by several suggested answers or completions. Select the one that BEST answers the question or completes the statement. *PRINT THE LETTER OF THE CORRECT ANSWER IN THE SPACE AT THE RIGHT.*

1. VoIP allows sending voice data using
   - A. fiber optics
   - B. PSTN
   - C. standard IP
   - D. copper wires

   1._____

2. Bootstrapping refers to the _____ process.
   - A. self-starting
   - B. batch processing
   - C. infinite
   - D. automatically ending

   2._____

3. NOS stands for Network
   - A. Operation Starter
   - B. On Standby
   - C. Optic Stream
   - D. Operating System

   3._____

4. Compared to LANs, WANS are more
   - A. reliable
   - B. congested
   - C. error-free
   - D. cheaper

   4._____

5. The initial setup costs for LAN are _____ compared to WAN.
   - A. the same
   - B. low
   - C. high
   - D. very high

   5._____

6. WANs are often built using
   - A. more than one adjacent LAN
   - B. leased lines
   - C. fiber optic cables
   - D. extranet

   6._____

7. The operating and maintenance costs of WAN are _____ compared to LAN.
   - A. very low
   - B. low
   - C. high
   - D. very high

   7._____

8. Nowadays, most LAN(s) use _____ as standard.
   - A. Ethernet
   - B. VPN over Internet
   - C. frame relay
   - D. leased lines

   8._____

9. WANs may use _____ as standard.
   - A. Ethernet
   - B. Subnet
   - C. VPN
   - D. Fast Ethernet

   9._____

10. A computer network spanning three university campuses within remote geographical locations is a typical example of a _____ area network.
    - A. campus
    - B. wide
    - C. metropolitan
    - D. local

    10._____

11. Client server networks require a _____ server.
    - A. dedicated
    - B. parallel
    - C. data
    - D. file

    11._____

12. A file server will typically run _____ protocol.
    - A. HTTP
    - B. IP
    - C. HTTPs
    - D. FTP

    12._____

66

13. _____ servers allow central administration of user and network resources.
    A. Print   B. Directory   C. File   D. Application

14. Network resources will be optimally used from a central resource in a _____ computer network model.
    A. central   B. distributed   C. remote   D. wireless

15. An internetwork will connect at least two
    A. internets   B. extranets   C. intranets   D. networks

16. Internet Protocol Security (IPSec) is a(n) _____ part of the IPV4.
    A. optional   B. integral/mandatory
    C. built-in   D. missing

17. Features of _____ can be extended by adding headers.
    A. IPV4   B. IPV6   C. IP   D. TCP

18. The available types of communication in IPV4 are unicast, multicast and
    A. podcast   B. broadcast   C. lancast   D. delicast

19. In backup terminology, a cold site means
    A. needs time to switch to normal operations
    B. readily available backup
    C. a backup on Cloud
    D. a separate backup

20. An overlapping frame is called a(n)
    A. header   B. packet
    C. collision   D. extended frame

21. _____ is a set of checks/rules for communication.
    A. Protocol   B. Syntax
    C. Lexical grammar   D. Encryption

22. Multiplexing collects data from different
    A. networks   B. applications   C. addresses   D. routers

23. When a block of data is transmitted, supplement data is attached to the _____ for use from one layer to another.
    A. datagram   B. packet   C. FIN bit   D. header

24. De-multiplexing is done in a(n) _____ layer.
    A. transport   B. network   C. data   D. application

25. In large networks, a _____ will divide the network into logical parts called segments to handle data traffic.
    A. switch   B. hub   C. router   D. bridge

KEY (CORRECT ANSWERS)

1. C
2. A
3. D
4. B
5. B

6. B
7. C
8. A
9. C
10. C

11. A
12. D
13. C
14. A
15. D

16. B
17. B
18. B
19. A
20. C

21. A
22. B
23. D
24. A
25. C

EXAMINATION SECTION
TEST 1

DIRECTIONS: Each question or incomplete statement is followed by several suggested answers or completions. Select the one that BEST answers the question or completes the statement. *PRINT THE LETTER OF THE CORRECT ANSWER IN THE SPACE AT THE RIGHT.*

1. _____ computer(s) can transmit data at a time in a network.
   A. Sender and the receiver
   B. Only one
   C. All
   D. Selected

2. Switching networks are also called _____ networks.
   A. streaming   B. transmission   C. packet   D. routing

3. Data may be lost in transmission. _____ will help the transmitter and receiver to determine correctly received data.
   A. Fair use
   B. Coordination
   C. Packet layers
   D. Correction bit

4. A network has a capacity of 3 minutes to transfer a file of 3 MB. Therefore,
   A. a 3 MB file is always transferred in 3 minutes
   B. priority transfer time is 3 minutes for a 3 MB file
   C. network congestion is no more than 3 minutes
   D. wait time for each new transfer is 3 minutes

5. While a 3 MB file is being transmitted, a 3 KB file is added for transmission.
   A. 3 MB file will be sent in the same time as previous
   B. 3 MB file is delayed
   C. 3 KB file is delayed
   D. There is no effect on transmission time

6. All packets enter the transmission medium at
   A. demultiplexor   B. multiplexor   C. hub   D. switch

7. Packet size
   A. must be standard for all hardware technologies
   B. targets the format of the frame used
   C. varies with the hardware used
   D. depends on the type of transmission medium

8. Frame has a
   A. begin bit and end bit
   B. start and stop bit
   C. header and trailer
   D. predetermined size

9. Sending computer will transmit frame in this sequence:
   A. End (EOT), Header (SOH), Data
   B. Data and End (EOT)
   C. End (EOT), Data and Header (SOH)
   D. Header (SOH), Data and End (EOT)

10. EOT is missing. This indicates
    A. the sender crashed
    B. the receiver malfunctioned
    C. the packet was discarded
    D. transmission medium is faulty

11. A bad frame is detected. It will be
    A. resent
    B. corrected with a parity bit
    C. discarded
    D. transmitted with error bit

12. _____ is a technique to encode reserved bytes.
    A. Bit stuffing
    B. Encryption
    C. Modulation
    D. Encapsulation

13. _____ makes a pair of bytes from Reserved Byte.
    A. Receiver
    B. Sender
    C. Buffering algorithm
    D. Packet

14. Unwanted data is generated due to
    A. transmission errors
    B. incorrect frame format
    C. parity bit
    D. byte stuffing

15. Incorrect data is rejected during
    A. error correction
    B. demultiplexing
    C. multiplexing
    D. error detection

16. In 11100011, parity is
    A. even   B. odd   C. biased   D. checksum

17. One of the bits is changed from 0 to 1. The parity of resulting bits
    A. becomes undefined
    B. is wrong
    C. always changes to 0
    D. always changes to 1

18. _____ detects erroneous data.
    A. Sender after receiving error bit
    B. Error correction algorithm
    C. Packet
    D. Receiver based on parity

19. _____ is an error detection technique.
    A. CRC   B. CSMA   C. Byte stuffing   D. CMC

20. Checksum uses
    A. parity   B. redundancy   C. collision   D. sum of data

21. Unrolling loop is an _____ technique.
    A. optimization
    B. error detection
    C. error correction
    D. error

22. CRC stands for
    A. Core Recall Cycle
    B. Critical Recycle Code
    C. Coded Redundancy Check
    D. Cyclic Redundancy Check

23. CRC will follow
    A. SOH
    B. EOT
    C. parity bit
    D. error frame

24. In shared networks, data reaches _____ destination(s).
    A. selected
    B. all
    C. nearest node
    D. none of the above

25. Each station has a unique _____ address.
    A. frame
    B. hardware
    C. generic
    D. operational

KEY (CORRECT ANSWERS)

1.	B	11.	C
2.	C	12.	A
3.	B	13.	B
4.	D	14.	A
5.	A	15.	D
6.	B	16.	B
7.	C	17.	B
8.	C	18.	D
9.	D	19.	A
10.	A	20.	D

21. A
22. D
23. B
24. B
25. B

TEST 2

DIRECTIONS: Each question or incomplete statement is followed by several suggested answers or completions. Select the one that BEST answers the question or completes the statement. *PRINT THE LETTER OF THE CORRECT ANSWER IN THE SPACE AT THE RIGHT.*

1. _____ adds hardware address to outgoing frames.
   A. Byte stuffing B. CSMA C. DMA D. LAN interface
   1.____

2. _____ defines access rules.
   A. DMA B. CD/CSMA C. Parity bit D. Bit stuffing
   2.____

3. Each time a packet passes through the router, the number of _____ increases by 1.
   A. address bytes B. hops
   C. subnet masks D. processing cycles
   3.____

4. The hardware address is typically one to _____ bytes.
   A. four B. eight C. sixteen D. six
   4.____

5. _____ address is used to send messages to all stations.
   A. Broadcast B. Abstract C. Podcast D. Unique
   5.____

6. The data area following the header is called
   A. payload B. frame C. loader info D. packet
   6.____

7. An interface which receives all frames for analysis is
   A. DMA B. promiscuous mode
   C. NIC D. CSMA
   7.____

8. Analyzer can display real time info by
   A. capturing specific frames B. computing totals
   C. counting frames D. analyzing parity bits
   8.____

9. _____ can be used over a long distance.
   A. RS-232 B. Oscillating signal carriers
   C. Encoded signaling D. Beacon
   9.____

10. Carrier modulation can be used with _____ medium.
    A. fiber B. copper C. radio D. all types of
    10.____

11. _____ modulation involves timing shifts.
    A. Amplitude B. Frequency C. Phase shift D. TDM
    11.____

12. _____ is the responsibility of the modulator.
    A. Encoding of the data bits B. Decoding of data bits
    C. Transmission of the data D. Error detection in carrier
    12.____

13. Simultaneous _____ communication requires a modulator as well as a demodulator.
    A. half duplex   B. full duplex
    C. asynchronous   D. modulated

14. Transducers using modulation through sound use
    A. glass   B. dial-up   C. radio   D. copper

15. Air carries multiple signals called _____ for each TV station.
    A. frequency   B. amplitude   C. channels   D. modulations

16. Switching data streams sequentially is
    A. TDM   B. FDM   C. DTM   D. DMA

17. Network resources are managed using _____ service in Windows server-based networks.
    A. Windows active directory   B. Windows NT directory servicer
    C. NDM   D. DMS

18. IP subnets connected using fast links are called
    A. domain   B. controller   C. site   D. BDC

19. Object attributes in active directory are contained in
    A. configuration NC   B. CMD log
    C. MMC   D. Schema NC

20. For group policy objects, a folder exists on all domain controllers as
    A. SYSVOL   B. C$ C. $SYS   D. \\shared

21. A minimum required services and roles will run in
    A. minimal installation option   B. VMS
    C. server core   D. named piping

22. Minimum storage required for active directory is
    A. 100 MB   B. 200 MB   C. 250 MB   D. 512 MB

23. Administrators for duration of the schema update have the role of _____ Admins.
    A. Global   B. Schema   C. Security   D. Data

24. A site created when installed in a forest root domain controller will derive its name from
    A. default first site name   B. default site built in
    C. $wins   D. NC

25. A server that manages site-to-site replication is
    A. Bridgehead   B. Masthead   C. PDC   D. member

KEY (CORRECT ANSWERS)

1. D
2. B
3. B
4. D
5. A

6. A
7. B
8. B
9. B
10. D

11. D
12. A
13. B
14. B
15. C

16. A
17. A
18. C
19. D
20. A

21. C
22. B
23. B
24. A
25. A

TEST 3

DIRECTIONS: Each question or incomplete statement is followed by several suggested answers or completions. Select the one that BEST answers the question or completes the statement. *PRINT THE LETTER OF THE CORRECT ANSWER IN THE SPACE AT THE RIGHT.*

1. In Unix variants, _____ command is used to generate statistics on socket connections.
   A. SS   B. NETSTAT   C. IPNET   D. ST

2. The _____ command is used to send mail via SMTP server.
   A. MAILX   B. SMAIL   C. NETSND   D. CONM

3. Fdisk command on Linus is used to
   A. format hard disk
   B. check partition
   C. copy contents
   D. remove bad sectors

4. The _____ command is used to open the command prompt in Windows.
   A. LST   B. PRM   C. TASKMGR   D. CMD

5. IOS stands for
   A. Internet Operating System
   B. Internetwork Operating System
   C. Internal Operating System
   D. Input Output System

6. Which is TRUE of a switch connected in a star topology?
   A. Packets are sent to all recipients in the network
   B. Packets are sent to intended recipients
   C. Packets are filtered by the recipient
   D. Packets are filtered by the sender

7. Which is NOT an Ethernet cable standard?
   A. CAT-5   B. CAT-6   C. CAT-6e   D. CAT-5e

8. Ethernet cables physically differ by
   A. quality of material used
   B. number of twists per cm
   C. color coding scheme
   D. number of wire pairs

9. The term NEXT is used for
   A. lost packets   B. cable faults   C. parity   D. cross talk

10. A stranded cable is
    A. an unused cable
    B. loosely connected
    C. made up of multiple cables
    D. the main cause of communication error

11. Trusted Platform Module (TPM) is a(n)
    A. application software
    B. hardware chip
    C. Ethernet cabling standard
    D. encryption standard

12. Which statement is TRUE for BitLocker?
    A. It secures files one by one
    B. It secures the entire operating system
    C. It locks the entire drive
    D. It removes viruses

13. Web servers use _____ virtualization.
    A. server
    B. desktop
    C. application
    D. data

14. _____ is a Linux OS.
    A. CMOS
    B. VMS
    C. Novell
    D. Ubuntu

15. Wi-Fi means
    A. IEEE 802
    B. wireless fidelity
    C. wireless first
    D. SMPTE

16. _____ computing uses unused processing cycles from different computers.
    A. Cloud
    B. Network
    C. Packet
    D. Grid

17. The _____ command will be used to change file permissions.
    A. CHKDSK
    B. CHFLS
    C. CHMOD
    D. CHALP

18. CDFS is used for
    A. Window Active directory permissions
    B. making file system changes permanent
    C. checking for errors
    D. while reading CD-ROM

19. _____ is a technology provided for e-mail clients.
    A. Clutter
    B. NOVA
    C. ARPANET
    D. Outlook

20. Unix users are protected by a firewall service named
    A. TCP wrapper
    B. Fast TCP
    C. Modbus TCP/IP
    D. TOE

21. _____ mode allows troubleshooting of Windows critical errors.
    A. Safe
    B. Command line
    C. Line operation
    D. CHKLST

22. Protocol _____ allows multiple protocols to work together.
    A. stack
    B. pool
    C. block
    D. cloud

23. BCD is a data standard representing integers in _____ bits.
    A. 4
    B. 8
    C. 16
    D. 32

24. Copying digital content from a device of one type to another is   24.____
    A. space shifting   B. CODEC
    C. openshift   D. proportional spacing

25. A zero that exists on the leftmost digit of a number is   25.____
    A. significant   B. absolute   C. rounding   D. leading

KEY (CORRECT ANSWERS)

1.	A	11.	B
2.	A	12.	C
3.	B	13.	A
4.	D	14.	D
5.	B	15.	A
6.	B	16.	D
7.	B	17.	C
8.	B	18.	D
9.	D	19.	A
10.	C	20.	A

21.	A
22.	A
23.	A
24.	A
25.	D

TEST 4

DIRECTIONS: Each question or incomplete statement is followed by several suggested answers or completions. Select the one that BEST answers the question or completes the statement. *PRINT THE LETTER OF THE CORRECT ANSWER IN THE SPACE AT THE RIGHT.*

1. _____ interface allows a working based on body movements.
   A. Cyber   B. Nova   C. Rota   D. Haptic

2. Computers within the same domain acting as servers can have exactly _____ role(s).
   A. one   B. three   C. two   D. four

3. _____ is a part of an operating system.
   A. Kernel   B. Core   C. Grid   D. Cloud

4. File servers and application servers will typically be _____ servers in a Windows environment.
   A. data server   B. active directory   C. cluster   D. member

5. Any of the network computers can be the server in _____ network.
   A. client server   B. VLAN   C. peer-to-peer   D. terrestrial

6. Ad-hoc mode does NOT use any
   A. shared services   B. access point   C. protocol   D. data standards

7. Manchester encoding is a data _____ method.
   A. encryption   B. correction   C. compression   D. transmission

8. _____ server stores databases.
   A. File   B. Database   C. Data   D. Information

9. In a(n) _____ network, data may be coming from many sources but managed centrally.
   A. centralized   B. remote   C. distributed   D. isolated

10. Users outside of network are also allowed. They are part of the
    A. intranet   B. internet   C. subnet   D. extranet

11. Internet service providers are connected to each other using
    A. network access points (NAP)   B. access point (AP)
    C. APLink   D. virtual access points

12. An organization's network accessible to its staff only is a
    A. LAN   B. internet   C. intranet   D. WAN

13. _____ is memory area an application is legally allowed to access.
    A. Viber space   B. Address space
    C. Application memory   D. Physical memory

14. MAC OS always uses _____ addressing.
    A. segmented   B. thunking   C. flat   D. virtual

15. Multicast address is assigned to _____ device(s).
    A. one   B. any two specific
    C. NIC only   D. multiple

16. With _____, a packet can have multiple destinations.
    A. Mbone   B. MIDL   C. SDS   D. DDL

17. Rules and regulations governing the management of data are called
    A. computer law   B. compliance
    C. code law   D. GRC

18. An application in Windows that allows creating routing applications is
    A. RDMA   B. BRAS
    C. social routing   D. RRAS

19. A fiber-based distributed data interface will typically use _____ topology.
    A. star   B. mesh   C. bus   D. ring

20. The number of bits transferred from one device to another in 1 second is _____ rate.
    A. adaptive   B. bit   C. baud   D. passive

21. _____ is a scripting language used in Windows server OS, used for automating Windows management.
    A. Powershell   B. Vbscript   C. JDBC   D. JSON

22. What tool would you use for writing snap-ins in Windows?
    A. Powershell   B. WHS console
    C. APM   D. MMC

23. _____ monitors the packet collision rate.
    A. NIC   B. Switch   C. Router   D. API

24. Dynamic packet filtering is a feature of _____ architecture.
    A. firewall   B. DNA   C. FDDI   D. service

25. WHS denotes Windows
    A. hash system   B. home server
    C. hypertext service   D. help service

KEY (CORRECT ANSWERS)

1.	D		11.	B
2.	C		12.	C
3.	A		13.	B
4.	D		14.	C
5.	C		15.	D
6.	B		16.	A
7.	D		17.	B
8.	B		18.	D
9.	C		19.	D
10.	D		20.	B

21. A
22. D
23. C
24. A
25. B

EXAMINATION SECTION
TEST 1

DIRECTIONS: Each question or incomplete statement is followed by several suggested answers or completions. Select the one that BEST answers the question or completes the statement. *PRINT THE LETTER OF THE CORRECT ANSWER IN THE SPACE AT THE RIGHT.*

1. Cardinality in a relational model refers to numbers of
   A. tuples   B. attributes   C. tables   D. constraints

2. The "AS" clause in SQL is used for which operation?
   A. Selection   B. Rename   C. Join   D. Projection

3. Database code is written in
   A. HLL   B. DML   C. DDL   D. DCL

4. In a hierarchical model, records are organized in
   A. graph   B. list   C. links   D. tree

5. In the entity integrity, the primary key has the value
   A. not null
   B. null
   C. both null and not null
   D. any value

6. The tuple relational calculus P1®P2 stands for
   A. ¬P1 Ú P2   B. P1 Ú P2   C. P1 Ù P2   D. P1 Ù¬P2

7. The method of key transformation is known as
   A. direct   B. hash   C. random   D. sequential

8. The file organization with fast access to any arbitrary record of a file is
   A. ordered file
   B. unordered file
   C. hashed file
   D. B-tree

9. In E-R diagram attributed is symbolized by
   A. ellipse
   B. dashed ellipse
   C. rectangle
   D. triangle

10. The operator used to compare a value to a list of literal values is
    A. BETWEEN   B. ANY   C. IN   D. ALL

11. B-tree of order m has maximum children of
    A. m   B. m+1   C. m-1   D. m/2

12. The function that divides one numeric expression by another and returns the remainder is
    A. POWER   B. MOD   C. ROUND   D. REMAINDER

13. A reflexive association is drawn by
    A. a line
    B. small open diamond
    C. small closed diamond
    D. small triangle at the end of a line

14. The special association that indicates multiple textbooks with a course is _____ association.
    A. aggregation
    B. generalization
    C. n-ary
    D. reflexive

15. In a reflexive association, one class is
    A. broken down into special cases
    B. combined with multiple other classes
    C. combined with one other class
    D. linked back to itself

16. The technique of defining common properties or functions in the higher class and then modifying them in the lower classes is called
    A. inheritance
    B. polymorphism
    C. reflexive
    D. transformance

17. Hiding manager's information from the employees is data hiding at
    A. conceptual level
    B. physical level
    C. external level
    D. none of the above

18. Versatile report provides
    A. columnar totals
    B. subtotals
    C. calculations
    D. all of the above

19. A locked file is
    A. accessed by one user
    B. modified by users having passwords
    C. used to hide sensitive information
    D. both B and C

20. The SQL command that modifies the rows of tables is known as
    A. update   B. insert   C. browse   D. append

21. Which one is NOT an aggregate function?
    A. AVG   B. SUM   C. UPPER   D. MAX

22. In replacing the relation section with some other relation, the initial step is
    A. delete section
    B. drop section
    C. delete from section
    D. replace section with new table

23. Which is NOT a relational database?
    A. dBase IV
    B. 4th Dimension
    C. FoxPro
    D. Reflex

24. A grouped report is a type of report
    A. generated by the Report Wizard
    B. that presents records sorted in ascending or descending order as you specify
    C. that displays data grouped by fields you specify
    D. none of the above

    24.____

25. The output of (100202,Drake,Biology,30000) is
    A. row(s) inserted
    B. error in ID of insert
    C. error in name of insert
    D. error in salary of the insert

    25.____

KEY (CORRECT ANSWERS)

1.	A		11.	A
2.	B		12.	B
3.	C		13.	B
4.	D		14.	D
5.	A		15.	D
6.	B		16.	B
7.	B		17.	C
8.	C		18.	D
9.	B		19.	A
10.	A		20.	A

21.	C
22.	B
23.	D
24.	C
25.	B

TEST 2

DIRECTIONS: Each question or incomplete statement is followed by several suggested answers or completions. Select the one that BEST answers the question or completes the statement. *PRINT THE LETTER OF THE CORRECT ANSWER IN THE SPACE AT THE RIGHT.*

1. The name of a procedural language is
   - A. domain relational calculus
   - B. tuple relational calculus
   - C. relational algebra
   - D. query language

   1.____

2. The statement Select* from employee is
   - A. DML
   - B. DDL
   - C. View
   - D. Integrity constraint

   2.____

3. The Delete from r; r-relation will
   - A. remove relation
   - B. clear relation entries
   - C. delete fields
   - D. delete rows

   3.____

4. The embedded SQL in COBOL is
   - A. EXEC SQL;
   - B. EXEC SQL END-EXEC
   - C. EXEC SQL
   - D. EXEC SQL END EXEC;

   4.____

5. Protocols that ensure conflict safety from deadlocks are
   - A. two-phase locking protocol
   - B. time-stamp ordering protocol
   - C. graph based protocol
   - D. both A and B above

   5.____

6. To reduce the process time of remote backup, we use
   - A. flags
   - B. breakpoints
   - C. redo points
   - D. checkpoints

   6.____

7. Sort and Filter group commands are in the _____ ribbon.
   - A. Home   B. Create   C. Tools   D. Fields

   7.____

8. The options Relationship and SQL Server are placed in the _____ tab.
   - A. External Data
   - B. Database Tools
   - C. Create
   - D. Home

   8.____

9. You cannot drop a table if a Drop Table has a constraint of the _____ key.
   - A. local   B. primary   C. composite   D. foreign

   9.____

10. Transaction can persist crashes by using the property of
    - A. atomicity
    - B. durability
    - C. isolation
    - D. all of the above

    10.____

11. Integrity constraints are defined in the language
    - A. DDL Right
    - B. DCL
    - C. DML
    - D. none of the above

    11.____

12. A group of commands collectively performing a function is
    A. procedure
    B. transaction right!
    C. query
    D. function

13. Poor administration of data leads to
    A. same data entity with single definition
    B. familiarity of existing data
    C. data elements missing
    D. all of the above

14. The intrusion detection system does not perform
    A. identification of hacking attempt into a system
    B. monitoring transfer of packets over the network
    C. transmitting the message packets to destination
    D. establishing deception systems to trap hackers

15. Hypertext Transfer Protocol (HTTP) defines the
    A. protocol to copy files between computers
    B. transfer protocol to transfer web pages to a browser
    C. database access protocol for SQL statements
    D. hardware/software protocol that limits access to company data

16. A CASE SQL statement defines
    A. an IF-THEN-ELSE in SQL
    B. a loop in SQL
    C. data definition in SQL
    D. all of the above

17. Routines and triggers define
    A. procedural code
    B. a call to operate
    C. automatic run
    D. storage in the database

18. To join tables, we take the approach of
    A. subqueries
    B. union join
    C. natural join
    D. all of the above

19. Backward recovery defines
    A. before-images applied to the database
    B. after-images applied to the database
    C. after-images and before-images applied to the database
    D. switching to an existing copy of the database

20. Locking may cause
    A. erroneous updates
    B. deadlock
    C. versioning
    D. all of the above

21. After a system failure, you recover a database through
    A. rollback
    B. rollforward
    C. switch to duplicate database
    D. reprocess transactions

22. Read-only databases are _____ updated.
    A. always   B. commonly   C. seldom   D. never

23. In order to secure a database, an administrative policy must consider
    A. authentication policies
    B. limiting access to only authorized people
    C. ensuring appropriate response rates are in external maintenance agreements
    D. all of the above

24. Data management technology does not include
    A. relational   B. rational
    C. object-oriented   D. dimensional

25. SQL INSERT statement defines
    A. rows modified according to criteria only
    B. mass of rows which cannot be copied from one table to another only
    C. rows inserted into a table only one at a time
    D. rows inserted into a table one at a time or in groups

KEY (CORRECT ANSWERS)

1.	C	11.	A
2.	A	12.	B
3.	C	13.	C
4.	B	14.	C
5.	B	15.	B
6.	D	16.	A
7.	A	17.	A
8.	B	18.	D
9.	D	19.	A
10.	B	20.	B

21.	C
22.	D
23.	D
24.	B
25.	D

TEST 3

DIRECTIONS: Each question or incomplete statement is followed by several suggested answers or completions. Select the one that BEST answers the question or completes the statement. *PRINT THE LETTER OF THE CORRECT ANSWER IN THE SPACE AT THE RIGHT.*

1. Which one is NOT a component of a database?
   A. User data B. Metadata C. Reports D. Indexes

2. The commercial website Amazon.com is an example of _____ database application.
   A. single-user
   B. multi-user
   C. e-commerce
   D. data mining

3. Which of the following products was the FIRST to implement true relational algebra in a PC DBMS?
   A. IDMS B. Oracle C. dBase-II D. R:base

4. SQL stands for _____ Language.
   A. Structured Query
   B. Sequential Query
   C. Structured Question
   D. Sequential Question

5. DBMS function is not used to
   A. create and process forms
   B. create databases
   C. process data
   D. administer databases

6. Which function assists people to keep track of their things?
   A. Database B. Table C. Instance D. Relationship

7. In an ODBC environment, a mediator between application and the DBMS drivers is
   A. data source
   B. driver
   C. driver manager
   D. OLE DB

8. An Enterprise Resource Planning application is a(n) _____ database application.
   A. single-user
   B. multi-user
   C. e-commerce
   D. data mining

9. The use of ID-dependent entities defines
   A. association relationships only
   B. multi-valued attributes only
   C. archetype/instance relationships only
   D. all of the above use ID dependent entities

10. The entity identifier in a table is
    A. foreign key
    B. main attribute
    C. primary key
    D. identity key

11. Which is FALSE for surrogate keys?
    A. They are short
    B. They are fixed
    C. They have meaning to the user
    D. They are numeric

12. Minimum cardinalities for every relationship is
    A. two   B. three   C. four   D. six

13. VPD provides authorization, and the mechanism is called
    A. row-level authorization
    B. column-level authorization
    C. row-type authentication
    D. authorization security

14. ON UPDATE CASCADE ensures
    A. normalization
    B. data integrity
    C. materialized views
    D. all of the above

15. SQL for an index is
    A. CREATE INDEX ID;
    B. CHANGE INDEX ID;
    C. ADD INDEX ID;
    D. REMOVE INDEX ID;

16. The sub-query bracket of an SQL SELECT statement is
    A. Braces – {...}
    B. CAPITAL LETTERS
    C. parenthesis – (...)
    D. brackets – [...]

17. Five built-in functions provided by SQL are
    A. COUNT, SUM, AVG, MAX, MIN
    B. SUM, AVG, MIN, MAX, MULT
    C. SUM, AVG, MULT, DIV, MIN
    D. SUM, AVG, MIN, MAX, NAME

18. The Microsoft Access wildcards are
    A. asterisk (*); percent sign (%)
    B. percent sign (%); underscore (_)
    C. underscore (_); question mark (?)
    D. question mark (?); asterisk (*)

19. The function used to sort rows in SQL is
    A. SORT BY
    B. ALIGN BY
    C. ORDER BY
    D. GROUP BY

20. EXISTS keyword defines
    A. only one row in the sub-query meets the condition
    B. all rows in the sub-query fail the condition
    C. both A and B
    D. none of the above

21. In SQL Server 2000, the parameters used in stored procedures are indicated with
    A. #   B. %   C. &   D. @

22. Trigger supported by SQL Server is
    A. INSTEAD OF only
    B. AFTER only
    C. BEFORE only
    D. INSTEAD OF and AFTER only

23. Which function in SQL Server 2000 tracks copy of changes since the last backup in the database?
    A. Complete backup
    B. Transaction log
    C. Differential backup
    D. None of the above

24. The transaction log defines the ____ of a record.
    A. before-image
    B. after-image
    C. before and after-image
    D. essential data

25. Database is recovered by
    A. rollback
    B. rollforward
    C. switch to duplicate database
    D. reprocess transactions

KEY (CORRECT ANSWERS)

1.	C	11.	C
2.	C	12.	D
3.	D	13.	A
4.	A	14.	B
5.	A	15.	A
6.	A	16.	C
7.	C	17.	A
8.	B	18.	D
9.	D	19.	C
10.	C	20.	A

21.	D
22.	D
23.	C
24.	D
25.	C

TEST 4

DIRECTIONS: Each question or incomplete statement is followed by several suggested answers or completions. Select the one that BEST answers the question or completes the statement. *PRINT THE LETTER OF THE CORRECT ANSWER IN THE SPACE AT THE RIGHT.*

1. A relational database includes a collection of
   A. tables   B. fields   C. records   D. keys

1.____

2. A domain is said to be atomic if elements are
   A. different   B. indivisible   C. constant   D. divisible

2.____

3. The statement Course(course_id,sec_id,semester) course_id,sec_id and semester are defined as
   A. relations, attribute   B. attributes, relation
   C. tuple, relation   D. tuple, attributes

3.____

4. Each entity has a descriptive property called
   A. entity   B. attribute   C. relation   D. model

4.____

5. The structure of the relation, deleting relation, and relating schemas is defined in
   A. DML (Data Manipulation Language)
   B. DDL (Data Definition Language)
   C. Query
   D. Relational Schema

5.____

6. To query information and to insert tuples, delete tuples, and modify tuples we use
   A. DML (Data Manipulation Language)
   B. DDL (Data Definition Language)
   C. Query
   D. Relational Schema

6.____

7. Which function is used to remove a relation from an SQL database?
   A. Delete   B. Purge   C. Remove   D. Drop Table

7.____

8. Insert into instructor values (10211,'Smith','Biology',66000); defines
   A. Query   B. DML   C. Relational   D. DDL

8.____

9. To append two strings, we use operator
   A. &   B. %   C. || D. _

9.____

10. In the DBMS environment, Date format is
   A. mm/dd/yy   B. yyyy/mm/dd   C. dd/mm/yy   D. yy/dd/mm

10.____

11. SQL store movie and image files by data type:
    A. clob   B. blob   C. binary   D. image

12. Hashing search defines _____ time.
    A. O(1)   B. O(n2)   C. O(log n)   D. O(n log n)

13. Key value pairs defines
    A. hash tables   B. heaps   C. both A and B   D. skip list

14. Breadth First Search is
    A. binary trees
    B. stacks
    C. graphs
    D. both A and C above

15. We identify deleted records by _____ bitmap.
    A. existence   B. current   C. final   D. deleted

16. The oldest database model is
    A. relational   B. deductive   C. physical   D. network

17. Snapshot isolation defines
    A. concurrency-control
    B. concurrency-allowance
    C. redirection
    D. repetition-allowance

18. A condition in SQL is
    A. join in SQL
    B. join condition
    C. both of the above
    D. none of the above

19. The operation allowed in a join view is
    A. UPDATE
    B. INSERT
    C. DELETE
    D. all of the above

20. Concurrency control on B+ trees is used to
    A. remove unwanted data
    B. easily add the index elements
    C. maintain accuracy of index
    D. all of the above

21. The protocol locking while crabbing goes
    A. down the tree and back up
    B. up the tree and back down
    C. down the tree and releases
    D. up the tree and releases

22. To reduce overhead and retrieve records from storage we use
    A. logs
    B. log buffer
    C. medieval space
    D. lower records

23. The space on disk allocated by the operating system for storing virtual-memory pages are called
    A. latches
    B. swap space
    C. dirty block
    D. none of the above

24. In two-factor authentication, the users can face an attack called   24._____
    A. radiant   B. cross attack
    C. scripting   D. man-in-the-middle

25. The attack that force an application to execute an SQL query is called   25._____
    A. SQL injection   B. SQL   C. direct   D. application

KEY (CORRECT ANSWERS)

1. A   11. B
2. B   12. A
3. B   13. A
4. B   14. C
5. B   15. A

6. A   16. D
7. D   17. A
8. B   18. B
9. C   19. D
10. B   20. C

21. A
22. B
23. B
24. D
25. A

EXAMINATION SECTION
TEST 1

DIRECTIONS: Each question or incomplete statement is followed by several suggested answers or completions. Select the one that BEST answers the question or completes the statement. *PRINT THE LETTER OF THE CORRECT ANSWER IN THE SPACE AT THE RIGHT.*

1. Which of the following languages could be used for the programming of a mobile application?
   A. C++
   B. Java
   C. PHP
   D. A and B only

   1.____

2. Which version of the iOS supports multitasking?
   A. All versions
   B. iOS4 and above
   C. iOS4
   D. None

   2.____

3. In iOS, _____ control(s) the presentation of an app's content on the screen.
   A. UI controller
   B. view controller objects
   C. UI objects
   D. controller objects

   3.____

4. _____ are important considerations for mobile applications.
   A. Business case and platform
   B. USP and SDK
   C. SDK and business case
   D. Emulator and SDK

   4.____

5. A mobile application can access
   A. application specific data
   B. personal and device location data
   C. device location
   D. application specific data, personal and device location data

   5.____

6. AAPT is a packaging tool specifically used for
   A. Android
   B. iOS
   C. Windows phone
   D. both A and B

   6.____

7. Android architecture is composed of _____ key components.
   A. five
   B. three
   C. two
   D. four

   7.____

8. ADB is associated only with
   A. iOS
   B. Android
   C. both A and B
   D. Windows

   8.____

9. Does the iPhone browser support Flash files?
   A. Yes
   B. No
   C. Only those developed by Apple
   D. Specific versions

   9.____

10. On Apple devices, Facetime is associated with
    A. digital photos
    B. video calls
    C. editing photos
    D. taking videos

10.____

11. If a mobile application is not working, what should be considered FIRST?
    A. Troubleshooting through application page
    B. Add notifications
    C. Both A and B
    D. Restart the device

11.____

12. X-code can be used only in
    A. iOS
    B. OS X
    C. Android
    D. Both A and B

12.____

13. Setting permission is important in mobile application development because permission applies restrictions on
    A. data
    B. code
    C. both A and B
    D. the device

13.____

14. On an Apple device, while registering the app, sometimes the configuration profile fails to install because
    A. there is no Internet access
    B. the app cannot connect to the HCP
    C. the app version on the mobile device is not supported by the application server
    D. the user is trying to register with a different HCP

14.____

15. Some of the well-known issues associated with iOS include
    A. Quick type, Facetime and save messages
    B. Facetime and hanging of applications
    C. Save messages and video sharing
    D. Quick type and sending files

15.____

16. If the file viewer is experiencing an error, what is a possible solution?
    A. Turn off the device
    B. Initiate Airplane Mode
    C. Turn off>turn on>view file again
    D. Turn on Wi-Fi

16.____

17. Which of the following is a likely reason that a mobile app cannot connect to the HCP system?
    A. No Internet access
    B. SSL server certificate
    C. Both A and B
    D. Application is expired

17.____

18. Which of the following JSON framework is supported by IOS?
    A. SBJson
    B. Ajax
    C. Json-rpc
    D. Both A and C

18.____

19. Which of the following frameworks is used to construct application user's interface for iOS?
    A. UIKit framework
    B. SDK
    C. IOS SDK
    D. Both A and C

20. What are the tools required to develop iOS applications?
    A. Intel-based Macintosh computer
    B. iOS SDK
    C. Both A and B
    D. SDK

21. In iOS, UIWindow object is responsible for the presentation of
    A. single view
    B. multiple views
    C. screen
    D. icon only

22. Android displays a status for non-responsive applications which is named as
    A. ANR   B. NRA   C. RAN   D. both A and B

23. Android debug bridge specifically controls
    A. intent filters
    B. icons and labels
    C. permissions
    D. communication concerning emulator port

24. In Android application development, intent is used to start a new
    A. activity   B. class   C. instance   D. both A and B

25. Which one of the following is the MOST popular language for Android applications?
    A. Java   B. Asp.Net   C. PHP   D. Object pascal

KEY (CORRECT ANSWERS)

1.	D	11.	C
2.	D	12.	D
3.	B	13.	C
4.	A	14.	A
5.	D	15.	A
6.	A	16.	C
7.	D	17.	C
8.	B	18.	A
9.	A	19.	A
10.	B	20.	C

21. B
22. A
23. D
24. A
25. A

TEST 2

DIRECTIONS: Each question or incomplete statement is followed by several suggested answers or completions. Select the one that BEST answers the question or completes the statement. *PRINT THE LETTER OF THE CORRECT ANSWER IN THE SPACE AT THE RIGHT.*

1. In general, mobile application development life cycle consists of _____ phase(s).
    A. five   B. four   C. three   D. one

2. Xamarin offers single language C#, which could be used for
    A. Android, iOS, Windows phone
    B. iOS
    C. Windows phone and Symbian
    D. iOS and Windows phone

3. Which of the following is included in Xamarin?
    A. Modern Language Constructs   B. Amazing Base Class Library
    C. Web services   D. Both A and B

4. Which one of the following is the BEST choice to develop cross-platform mobile applications?
    A. Xamarin   B. Objective-C
    C. Swift and Java   D. PHP

5. SQLite database engine is used for _____-based mobile applications.
    A. iOS   B. Android
    C. iOS and Android   D. Symbian

6. The MOST basic function of Portable Class Library is to
    A. distribute assemblies   B. build assemblies
    C. create cross-platform solution   D. both A and B

7. Mobile applications which are built using Xamarin also use _____ web services.
    A. REST, SOUP and WCF   B. SOUP
    C. WCF and REST   D. all of the above

8. Which of the following commercial services are used for notifications in mobile applications?
    A. Urban Airship   B. Windows Azure
    C. PushSharp   D. A and B only

9. iOS and _____ provide means for interpreting patterns of touches into gestures.
    A. Android   B. Symbian   C. Windows   D. Blackberry

10. Assets folder created for Android includes _____ files.   10._____
    A. Text, font, XML, audio and video   B. XML
    C. music and video   D. HTML

11. Android asset packaging tools deal with   11._____
    A. zip compatible archives   B. cross-platform applications
    C. storage   D. B and C only

12. In Android environment, which one of the following describes the purpose   12._____
    of Emulator?
    A. Write code + test code
    B. Debug code + test code + write code
    C. Test code
    D. Write code

13. Store Kit APIs are used to sell digital products and services only in   13._____
    A. iOS   B. Android   C. Symbian   D. both A and B

14. Which one of the following is the MOST acceptable use of images in iOS   14._____
    applications?
    A. Resolution independent images
    B. Asset catalog, image sets, images in code, resolution independent
       images
    C. Images in code
    D. Both A and C

15. On Android devices, when multiple files are sent to another app, some files   15._____
    could not be downloaded. This is because
    A. the app cannot connect to the HCP
    B. one or more files have larger size than the limit
    C. HCP is not responding
    D. A and B only

16. When the file viewer is experiencing an error, what is the possible outcome?   16._____
    A. File content is blank   B. File sending is failed
    C. Both A and B   D. File becomes corrupt

17. If the storage quota has been exceeded, what are the possible solutions?   17._____
    A. Delete and remove files from synced folder
    B. Increase storage quota by asking administrator
    C. Both A and B
    D. Buy memory card

18. What is the purpose of containers in Android applications?   18._____
    A. Hold objects and widgets   B. ProgressDialog
    C. Assist in display   D. Notifications

19. Android application architecture is based on
    A. intent
    B. resource
    C. notification
    D. content providers

    19.____

20. Which one of the following is a storage method for Android?
    A. SQLite database
    B. MYSQL
    C. SQL2008
    D. Both A and B

    20.____

21. Android Open-source project is responsible to maintain
    A. new versions and compatibility
    B. Android software and cross-platform support
    C. compatibility
    D. Cross-platform support

    21.____

22. Which one of the following is related to the iOS?
    A. Multitasking, SBJson, UIKit framework
    B. SBJson
    C. UIKit framework
    D. Multitasking

    22.____

23. Which API in iOS is used to write test scripts that assist the running of an application's user interface elements?
    A. UI Automation API
    B. UI API
    C. Automation API
    D. Both A and B

    23.____

24. An application in iOS is an active application when it is
    A. receiving events
    B. running in foreground
    C. running in background
    D. both A and B

    24.____

25. In iOS, UIKit classes could be used by
    A. all threads
    B. application's main thread
    C. single thread
    D. both A and B

    25.____

KEY (CORRECT ANSWERS)

1. A
2. A
3. D
4. A
5. C

6. D
7. A
8. D
9. A
10. A

11. A
12. B
13. A
14. B
15. D

16. C
17. C
18. A
19. D
20. A

21. A
22. A
23. A
24. D
25. B

EXAMINATION SECTION
TEST 1

DIRECTIONS: Each question or incomplete statement is followed by several suggested answers or completions. Select the one that BEST answers the question or completes the statement. *PRINT THE LETTER OF THE CORRECT ANSWER IN THE SPACE AT THE RIGHT.*

1. Which of the following is NOT a step of Information System Audit Process?
   A. Planning
   B. Studying/Testing and Evaluating Controls
   C. Interfacing
   D. Reporting

2. Controlled disclosure of information is known as
   A. privacy   B. security   C. integrity   D. confidentiality

3. The maintenance of fault tolerance, DR, backup and storage procedures falls under _____ Review.
   A. Network Security
   B. Business Continuity
   C. Data Integrity
   D. Environment

4. The document that contains the objectives, accountability and responsibility for the IS Audit is known as
   A. Audit Charter
   B. Software Charter
   C. Audit Report
   D. Audit Plan

5. Subject Matter Criteria should be
   A. subjective and objective
   B. objective and accountable
   C. objective and measurable
   D. complete and subjective

6. Which one of the following is NOT a step for Risk Management Process Area?
   A. Risk Ignorance
   B. Risk Measurement
   C. Risk Monitoring
   D. Risk Mitigation

7. Which is the correct sequence of IT Process Optimization steps?
   I. Identify and prioritize business process
   II. Finalize optimization techniques
   III. As-is process analysis
   IV. Implementation
   V. To-be process mapping

   The CORRECT answer is:
   A. I, II, III, IV, V
   B. I, III, II, V, IV
   C. I, III, IV, II, V
   D. I, II, IV, V, III

8. _____ is accountable for the internal IT and Environmental Organizational controls.
   A. Audit Committee
   B. Management
   C. Auditor
   D. Lead Auditor

9. COBIT Framework is referred to yield the organizational maturity in
   A. IT Governance
   B. IS Audit
   C. IS Security
   D. Audit Planning

10. Reviewing the extent of Project Management Techniques applied in an organization is done under _____ Planning.
    A. Strategic
    B. Business Strategic
    C. Audit
    D. Tactical

11. The document defining the justification of a project for its implementation is known as
    A. Project Plan
    B. Project Timeline
    C. Business Case
    D. Test Case

12. Incidence Reports should be reviewed during _____ Review.
    A. BCP
    B. Governance
    C. Business Case
    D. Network Security

13. Which is the missing testing phase among the following: Pretest; Post-test; Post-invocation?
    A. Preliminary Test
    B. Test
    C. Detailed Test
    D. Test Case

14. Measuring that the risk analysis is performed routinely is done under which aspect of BCP?
    A. Organizational
    B. Departmental
    C. Planning
    D. Procedural

15. Business Impact Analysis is performed before the implementation of
    A. Audit Planning
    B. Requirement Verification
    C. Business Continuity Plan
    D. Risk Assessment

16. Which phase is missing in the following list of SDLC phases: Business requirements definition; Design and development (construction); Testing; Implementation; Post-implementation?
    A. Business Case
    B. Project Initiation
    C. Project Maintenance
    D. Project Support

17. Requirement Sign-off is done under which phase?
    A. Project Initiation
    B. Implementation
    C. Post implementation
    D. Business requirements definition

18. A _____ is developed in order to maintain control of the project during its entire life cycle.
    A. Project Master Plan
    B. Project Scope Document
    C. Project Milestone
    D. Business Case

19. Which of the following plans covers the Issue Logging and Tracking?
    A. Project Plan
    B. Project Initiating Plan
    C. Risk Plan
    D. QA Plan

20. A feasibility study should involve the following: critical personnel, business personnel, QA personnel and
    A. management
    B. executive staff
    C. technical staff
    D. customers

21. Identification of telecommunication access paths into and out of the organization's premises is known as
    A. tracking
    B. rogue access jacks
    C. accessibility control
    D. routing control

22. Hard-coded MAC addresses lead to
    A. data loss
    B. incident reporting
    C. wireless vulnerability
    D. project issue

23. Encryption login credentials are used to maintain
    A. integrity
    B. accessibility
    C. confidentiality
    D. privacy

24. Assuring that data is not changed means
    A. integrity
    B. confidentiality
    C. security
    D. privacy

25. A very essential requirement for electronic payment is
    A. encryption
    B. nonrepudiation
    C. authentication
    D. authorization

KEY (CORRECT ANSWERS)

1. C
2. D
3. B
4. A
5. C

6. A
7. B
8. B
9. A
10. D

11. C
12. A
13. B
14. A
15. C

16. B
17. D
18. A
19. D
20. C

21. B
22. C
23. C
24. A
25. B

TEST 2

DIRECTIONS: Each question or incomplete statement is followed by several suggested answers or completions. Select the one that BEST answers the question or completes the statement. *PRINT THE LETTER OF THE CORRECT ANSWER IN THE SPACE AT THE RIGHT.*

1. Which of the following is NOT the main area for IS Audit?
   A. Availability
   B. Integrity
   C. Controllability
   D. Confidentiality

2. Which of the following provides a high level of assurance regarding the effectiveness of control procedures?
   A. Review
   B. Audit
   C. Peer Review
   D. Test

3. The internal audit plan must be approved by the
   A. auditor
   B. audit committee
   C. audit charter
   D. reviewer

4. Which of the following does NOT fall under the scope of the audit?
   A. People
   B. Date
   C. Application systems
   D. Inventory

5. _____ is known as the defined information in the auditor report and the procedures defining the controls operation and its compliance with IS Auditing Standards.
   A. Subject matter
   B. Subject report
   C. Subject criteria
   D. Audit charter

6. The process to check whether the Organization Mission and objective is aligned with the IS function is covered in
   A. Risk Assessment
   B. IT Governance
   C. Organizational Maturity Models
   D. Planning Guidelines

7. Application controls are defined as the grouped controls within
   A. application   B. software   C. hardware   D. organization

8. Data analysis techniques help to monitor the _____ of the system.
   A. robustness
   B. scalability
   C. extendibility
   D. reliability

9. The issues highlighted related to IT Governance must escalate to
   A. management
   B. higher management
   C. stakeholders/people
   D. auditors

10. The strategy to follow the measures that reduce the likelihood for a risk to occur is known as risk
    A. identification
    B. measurement
    C. management
    D. mitigation

11. Two parameters for risk management are
    A. likelihood and severity
    B. consequences and measures
    C. mitigation and likelihood
    D. severity and follow-up

12. Which one of the following is NOT a fundamental aspect of Benefits Realization Approach?
    A. Project Management
    B. Portfolio Management
    C. Service Catalog Management
    D. Full Cycle Governance

13. Which of the following is NOT a BCP Aspect of Review?
    A. Organizational
    B. Departmental
    C. Planning
    D. Procedural

14. What identifies the crucial recovery time frames of the critical business processes?
    A. Business impact analysis
    B. Business continuity
    C. Business case
    D. Business realization approaches

15. Planning of the periodic review of risk is done under which aspect of BCP?
    A. Organizational
    B. Planning
    C. Procedural
    D. Monitoring

16. When defining the system alternative solutions, which of the following should be given LEAST priority?
    A. System enhancements
    B. Manual solutions
    C. Vendor solutions
    D. In-house design and development

17. Verification of vendor agreements is done at
    A. business requirements definition
    B. design and development (construction)
    C. testing
    D. implementation

18. Legal and security requirements are identified during
    A. process audit
    B. requirement definition
    C. implementation
    D. support

19. A test plan should define which of the following roles for a test result?
    A. Reviewing and approver
    B. Author and reviewer
    C. Reviewer and manager
    D. Approver and author

3 (#2)

20. _____ review should be done to make sure that the project has met user expectations, project and timeline.
    A. QA
    B. Network
    C. Development
    D. Implementation

21. A system which validates that the public key belongs to the individual or organization is called the _____ system.
    A. KPI
    B. PKI
    C. SDLC
    D. testing

22. _____ is the way of authenticating the sending of a message.
    A. PKI
    B. Encryption
    C. Cryptography
    D. Digital signature

23. PKI stands for
    A. Public Key Infrastructure
    B. Private Key Infrastructure
    C. Public Key Identifier
    D. Private Key Identifier

24. Secure Sockets Layer/Transport Layer Security (SSL/TLS) is used for encryption of
    A. HTTP
    B. TCP
    C. UDP
    D. TTIP

25. The _____ digitally signs the certificate in order to validate that the public key belongs to the authorized owner.
    A. PKI
    B. KPI
    C. CA
    D. SSL

KEY (CORRECT ANSWERS)

1.	C		11.	A
2.	B		12.	C
3.	B		13.	B
4.	D		14.	A
5.	A		15.	B
6.	B		16.	B
7.	A		17.	A
8.	D		18.	B
9.	B		19.	A
10.	D		20.	D

21. B
22. D
23. A
24. A
25. C

EXAMINATION SECTION
TEST 1

DIRECTIONS: Each question or incomplete statement is followed by several suggested answers or completions. Select the one that BEST answers the question or completes the statement. *PRINT THE LETTER OF THE CORRECT ANSWER IN THE SPACE AT THE RIGHT.*

1. The "CIA Triad" stands for Confidentiality, Integrity and
   A. Availability
   B. Accessibility
   C. Authenticity
   D. Authorization

   1.____

2. _____ box is the testing type for which the intruder has no idea about the network.
   A. Black
   B. White
   C. Gray
   D. Green

   2.____

3. Which of the following IEEE standards is defined as the EAP over LAN?
   A. 802.1E
   B. 802.1Z
   C. 802.1Y
   D. 802.1X

   3.____

4. Which of the following applications is used to check for security holes in in the network?
   A. Logic bomb
   B. Log analyzer
   C. Vulnerability scanner
   D. Design reviewer

   4.____

5. _____ box is the type of testing in which the intruder has the network knowledge.
   A. Black
   B. White
   C. Gray
   D. Red

   5.____

6. On your network an alert is raised that an application is operating over it that has bypassed the authorization. This particular type of attack is known as
   A. DoS
   B. DDoS
   C. Backdoor
   D. Social engineering

   6.____

7. Your particular server does not acknowledge any TCP connections. It also suggests that the session limit has been exceeded. This particular type of attack is a
   A. TCP ACK attack
   B. Smurf attack
   C. Virus attack
   D. TCP/IP hijacking

   7.____

8. In a particular case where the system gets hanged to respond to the keyboard in a situation when the user has opened an Excel file and connected to the internet, this particular type of attack is known as
   A. logic bomb
   B. worm
   C. virus
   D. ACK attack

   8.____

109

9. You are working as the network analyst in a company. One of the company users called you because he has been receiving e-mails with a virus which are increasing in count and 200 come every day. What is this attack type?
   A. SAINT
   B. Backdoor
   C. Worm
   D. TCP/IP hijacking

10. An attacker's system looks like to be the server to the real client and appears to be the client as the real server. This type of attack is known as
    A. denial of service
    B. replay
    C. negative operational stability
    D. man-in-the-middle

11. RBAC stands for ____-based access control.
    A. role
    B. retro
    C. rational
    D. responsibility

12. To get the server backups, _____ authentication method would be ideal for this situation.
    A. MAC
    B. DAC
    C. RBAC
    D. security tokens

13. Which of the following concepts establishes a connection between two networks via secure protocol?
    A. Tunneling
    B. VLAN
    C. Internet
    D. Extranet

14. In the case where two or more parties authenticate each other, this condition is known as
    A. SSO
    B. multifactor authentication
    C. mutual authentication
    D. tunneling

15. Which aspect of physical security deals with the outer-level access control?
    A. Perimeter security
    B. Mantraps
    C. Security zones
    D. Locked door

16. _____ is an example of perimeter security.
    A. Chain link fence
    B. Video camera
    C. Elevator
    D. Locked computer room

17. _____ uses a physical characteristic in order to check for the identity.
    A. Surveillance
    B. Biometrics
    C. Smart Card
    D. CHAP authenticator

18. _____ is defined as the high-security installation that is based on the visual identification plus authentication for accessibility.
    A. Mantrap
    B. Fencing
    C. Proximity reader
    D. Hot aisle

19. PKI (Public Key Infrastructure) is defined as the key-asymmetric system that consists of _____ key(s).
    A. one
    B. two
    C. three
    D. four

20. Which of the following is the MOST widely used certificate?   20.____
    A. X.509   B. B.102   C. C.409   D. Z.602

21. Who of the following is responsible for issuing certificates?   21.____
    A. Registration authority (RA)   B. Certificate authority (CA)
    C. Document authority (DA)   D. Local registration authority (LRA)

22. Risk _____ is accomplished any time in order to take steps to reduce the risk.   22.____
    A. acceptance   B. avoidance   C. deterrence   D. mitigation

23. Risk _____ consists of identifying the enemy and warning him what harm   23.____
    he may get if he causes you harm.
    A. acceptance   B. avoidance   C. deterrence   D. mitigation

24. Risk _____ necessitates an identified risk and understands the possible   24.____
    cost/damage and agrees to accept.
    A. acceptance   B. avoidance   C. deterrence   D. mitigation

25. Risk _____ includes sharing a part of the burden of the risk with someone   25.____
    else.
    A. acceptance   B. avoidance   C. deterrence   D. transference

KEY (CORRECT ANSWERS)

1.	A	11.	A
2.	A	12.	C
3.	D	13.	A
4.	C	14.	C
5.	B	15.	A
6.	C	16.	A
7.	A	17.	B
8.	A	18.	A
9.	C	19.	B
10.	D	20.	A

21.	B
22.	D
23.	C
24.	A
25.	D

TEST 2

DIRECTIONS: Each question or incomplete statement is followed by several suggested answers or completions. Select the one that BEST answers the question or completes the statement. *PRINT THE LETTER OF THE CORRECT ANSWER IN THE SPACE AT THE RIGHT.*

1. _____ box is the type of testing in which the intruder is being given information from inside the network.
    A. Black B. White C. Gray D. Green

2. Which of the following is the type of testing that is performed from the intruder's perspective?
    A. Loop recon
    B. Flood gating
    C. Vulnerability scanning
    D. Penetration testing

3. What is the process that is used in order to check for holes in the custom applications?
    A. Network bridging
    B. Design review
    C. Code review
    D. Remediation

4. _____ is defined as the protection function that is embedded in firewalls, and used to tweak against unacknowledged log-in attacks.
    A. MAC filter
    B. Flood guard
    C. MAC limiter
    D. Security posture

5. Which of the following ways is used for establishing a secure connection between a web client and a web server?
    A. SSL/TSL and HTTPS
    B. TSL and ICMP
    C. SNMP and TCP
    D. HTTPS and HTTP

6. A certificate authority (CA) is defined as the organization which issues, revokes, as well as distributes which of the following?
    A. Tokens B. Licenses C. Certificates D. Tickets

7. Registration authority (RA) CANNOT perform which of the following?
    A. Distribute keys
    B. Accept registrations for the CA
    C. Validate identities
    D. Give recommendations

8. _____ is NOT one of the four main types of trust models used with PKI.
    A. Hierarchical B. Bridge C. Custom
    D. Mesh E. Hybrid

9. In a bridge trust model, which of the following types of relationships exists between the root CA's?
    A. Parent to child
    B. Peer to peer
    C. Father to daughter
    D. Sister to parent

10. Which of the following combinations (from top to bottom) lists the types of certificate servers that exist in a certificate hierarchy?
    A. CA, LRA, RA
    B. CA, RA, LRA
    C. RA, CA, LRA
    D. RA, LRA, CA

11. The MOST common certificate trust model is
    A. hierarchical
    B. bridge
    C. mesh (web of trust)
    D. hybrid

12. In a web session, the user enters the private information in a form page. Which protocol would be used for a secure session?
    A. SSL/TLS   B. SSH   C. IPSec   D. ISAKMP

13. The MAIN advantage of making use of decentralized/distributed key generation is
    A. more points of failure
    B. no single point of failure
    C. simpler key management
    D. more processing power required at the root server

14. When two people need to enter a password known only to them for a specific situation, what term defines requiring two people to perform a sensitive task?
    A. Separation of duties/dual control
    B. SLA
    C. Need to know
    D. Privacy

15. Which of the following helps to ensure confidentiality?
    A. Secure protocols
    B. The method used to deliver keys securely to their intended recipient
    C. Using hashing
    D. Using digital signatures

16. Which of the following entities impact the HIGHEST threat to network security?
    A. External hackers
    B. External crackers
    C. Internal threats
    D. Social engineering

17. A worm is defined as
    A. a self-replicating, self-contained chunk of malicious code
    B. a segment of code that waits for a certain condition to be true before it performs a malicious act
    C. an attack that prevents a legitimate client from receiving service
    D. a password-guessing algorithm

18. From the following, which ports are utilized by default for HTTP and HTTPS?
    A. 80, 443   B. 80, 448   C. 80, 883   D. 80, 433

19. What are two primary access control methods that are commonly combined in computer systems today?
    A. DAC and MAC
    B. MAC and RBAC
    C. RBAC and DAC
    D. SAC and MAC

    19._____

20. Which particular type of IPSec should be utilized for encryption on an LAN for internal security?
    A. Channeling
    B. Transport
    C. EAP
    D. L2TP

    20._____

21. When using asymmetric encryption where the data is encoded using a value of 5, _____ would be used to decode it.
    A. 5
    B. 1
    C. 1/5
    D. 0

    21._____

22. MAC is an acronym for
    A. media access control
    B. mandatory access control
    C. message authentication code
    D. multiple advisory committees

    22._____

23. Which document defines exactly how a CA issues certificates and their purpose?
    A. Certificate policies
    B. Certificate practices
    C. Revocation authority
    D. CRL

    23._____

24. _____ is similar to Blowfish but operates on 128-bit blocks.
    A. Twofish
    B. IDEA
    C. CCITT
    D. AES

    24._____

25. The specific process of deriving an encrypted value by making use of a mathematical process is known as
    A. hashing
    B. asymmetric
    C. symmetric
    D. social engineering

    25._____

KEY (CORRECT ANSWERS)

1. C
2. D
3. C
4. B
5. A

6. C
7. D
8. C
9. B
10. B

11. A
12. A
13. B
14. A
15. B

16. C
17. A
18. A
19. C
20. B

21. C
22. C
23. A
24. A
25. A

TEST 3

DIRECTIONS: Each question or incomplete statement is followed by several suggested answers or completions. Select the one that BEST answers the question or completes the statement. *PRINT THE LETTER OF THE CORRECT ANSWER IN THE SPACE AT THE RIGHT.*

1. The vulnerability scanner CANNOT be a
   A. port scanner
   B. network enumerator
   C. desktop application
   D. worm

   1.____

2. Which of the following is used in order to limit the damage by lessening the code amount?
   A. EAPOL
   B. EAP
   C. ASR
   D. 802.1X

   2.____

3. Nessus is a tool that operates on _____ security function.
   A. vulnerability scanning
   B. penetration testing
   C. ethical hacking
   D. loop protection

   3.____

4. Rule-based management is the method which describes the conditions for access to objects and is defined as
   A. distributed management
   B. management by objective
   C. role-based management
   D. label-based management

   4.____

5. Which of the following secure protocols should be used for FTP file transfers?
   A. ICMP
   B. TCP/IP
   C. SNMP
   D. SSH

   5.____

6. Which of the following is the term that is referred to as events that are by mistake identified as issues?
   A. Fool's gold
   B. Non-incidents
   C. Error flags
   D. False positives

   6.____

7. The component of risk assessment when used in a combination of _____ delivers an accurate image of any situation.
   A. RAC
   B. ALE
   C. BIA
   D. RMG

   7.____

8. Which of the following securities deal with network access control?
   A. Physical
   B. Operational
   C. Management
   D. Triad

   8.____

9. Which process is invoked when a person says that he is the user but is unable to be authenticated?
   A. Identity proofing
   B. Social engineering
   C. Directory traversal
   D. Cross-site requesting

   9.____

10. What is actually implied at the end of each access control list?
    A. Least privilege
    B. Separation of duties
    C. Implicit deny
    D. Explicit allow

    10.____

11. During the key recovery process, the ____ key has to be recoverable.
    A. rollover   B. secret   C. previous   D. escrow

12. The integrity part of security addresses which characteristic of information security?
    A. Verification that information is accurate
    B. Verification that ethics are properly maintained
    C. Establishment of clear access control of data
    D. Verification that data is kept private and secure

13. What is the main issue in using FTP servers?
    A. Password files are stored in an unsecured area on disk.
    B. Memory traces can corrupt file access.
    C. User ID's and passwords are unencrypted.
    D. FTP sites are unregistered.

14. Which of the following is the physical access device that is employed to restrict access to a small number of individuals at a given time?
    A. Checkpoint
    B. Perimeter security
    C. Security zones
    D. Mantrap

15. Which of the following is a set of voluntary standards governing encryption?
    A. PKI   B. PKCS   C. ISA   D. SSL

16. Which of the following encryption processes uses one message to hide another?
    A. Steganography
    B. Hashing
    C. MDA
    D. Cryptointelligence

17. _____ represents a security breach in a PKI environment.
    A. Access to a public key
    B. Disclosure of a private key
    C. Knowledge of a hash algorithm
    D. Copy of an encrypted file

18. Which of the following forms of cryptography is chiefly referred to as a one-way function?
    A. Asymmetric
    B. Hashing
    C. Digital signatures
    D. Symmetric

19. The algorithm which is referred to as the block cipher means that the algorithm is
    A. applied via an elliptical curve
    B. recursive
    C. symmetric
    D. asymmetric

20. Within the bridge trust model, a _____ relationship exists among the root CA's.
    A. parent to child
    B. peer to peer
    C. father to daughter
    D. sister to parent

21. In the _____ approach, the sending and receiving of both entities needs to have the same encryption key.
    A. applied via an elliptical key
    B. symmetric
    C. recursive
    D. asymmetric

22. Which of the following provides encryption for credit card numbers that can be transmitted over the internet?
    A. Secure Electronic Transaction (SET)
    B. SSL
    C. HTTPS
    D. TCP/IP

23. Which of the following devices provides infrastructure security at its best?
    A. Hub   B. Switch   C. Router   D. Modem

24. Which of the following bits are utilized in order to address with IPv4 and IPv6, respectively?
    A. 32,128   B. 16, 64   C. 8, 32   D. 4, 16

25. Which of the following protocols is unsuitable for WAN VPN connections?
    A. PPP   B. PPTP   C. L2TP   D. IPSec

KEY (CORRECT ANSWERS)

1.	C	11.	C
2.	C	12.	A
3.	A	13.	C
4.	D	14.	D
5.	D	15.	B
6.	D	16.	A
7.	B	17.	B
8.	B	18.	B
9.	A	19.	C
10.	C	20.	B

21.	B
22.	A
23.	C
24.	A
25.	A

TEST 4

DIRECTIONS: Each question or incomplete statement is followed by several suggested answers or completions. Select the one that BEST answers the question or completes the statement. *PRINT THE LETTER OF THE CORRECT ANSWER IN THE SPACE AT THE RIGHT.*

1. By reducing the tolerance of flood guard, which type of attacks can be reduced? 1.____
   A. Dos attacks
   B. Identify spoofing
   C. Eavesdropping
   D. Man in the Middle

2. The specific approach that is employed by a business for security concerns is 2.____
   A. rule-based management
   B. network bridging
   C. security posture
   D. assessment technique

3. Which of the following logs are NOT the logs used for network monitoring? 3.____
   A. Event B. Security C. Project D. Audit

4. _____ is used to manage a group or multicasting sessions' means to address multiple recipients for a data packet. 4.____
   A. Internet Group Management Protocol (IGMP)
   B. Simple Network Management Protocol (SNMP)
   C. Internet Control Message Protocol
   D. TCP/IP

5. _____ is used to manage and monitor devices, such as copiers, fax machines, and other smart office machines, over the network. 5.____
   A. Internet Group Management Protocol (IGMP)
   B. Simple Network Management Protocol (SNMP)
   C. Internet Control Message Protocol
   D. TCP/IP Protocol

6. LDAP is defined as an example of 6.____
   A. directory access protocol
   B. IDS
   C. tiered model application development environment
   D. file server

7. What particular kind of attack is made in order to overload a protocol or service? 7.____
   A. Spoofing
   B. Back door
   C. Man-in-the-Middle
   D. Flood

8. Which of the following provides extra security to the web server? 8.____
   A. Changing the port address to 80
   B. Changing the port address to 1019
   C. Adding a firewall to block port 80
   D. Web servers cannot be secured

9. What particular mechanism is employed in order to enable or disable access to a network resource based on an IP address?
   A. NDS B. ACL C. Hardening D. Port blocking

10. What is the MAIN objective of risk management?
    A. Reduce risk to an acceptable level
    B. Remove all risks from an environment
    C. Minimize security cost expenditures
    D. Assign responsibilities to job roles

11. Disaster recovery plans (DRP's) are dependent on
    A. insurance coverage
    B. risk assessment
    C. media spin management
    D. ethical backing

12. Which of the following is NOT a physical security control?
    A. Door locks
    B. Motion detectors
    C. Bulwark
    D. Strong passwords

13. Utilizing a smart card in order to offer a system with a user's private key is referred to as an act of
    A. authorization
    B. integrity verification
    C. sanitation
    D. authentication

14. To employ the single sign-on diminishes the need for
    A. account management systems
    B. strong passwords
    C. directory services
    D. multiple user names and passwords

15. Passwords are used for
    A. authentication
    B. authorization
    C. auditing
    D. access control

16. Which of the following is defined as the fastest method concerning encryption of a large amount of data?
    A. Symmetric cryptography
    B. Asymmetric cryptography
    C. Hashing
    D. Digitally signing

17. The process of binding a private key to its corresponding public key is the the function performed by
    A. digital signatures
    B. hashing
    C. evaluation criteria
    D. digital certificates

18. Which of the following is intended to prevent the unauthorized disclosure of information?
    A. Availability
    B. Authenticity
    C. Confidentiality
    D. Integrity

19. Which of the following validates the integrity of the message and the sender?
    A. IDS
    B. Digital signatures
    C. Public key
    D. Private key

20. Which of the following is the physical access method in which a dumpster contains sensitive information?
    A. Dumpster diving
    B. DoS
    C. Man-in-the-Middle
    D. Worm

21. Pretty Good Privacy (PGP) is a freeware _____ encryption system.
    A. storage
    B. file
    C. e-mail
    D. network

22. Certificate Management Protocol (CMP) is a messaging protocol used between _____ entities.
    A. private key
    B. public key
    C. IDS
    D. PKI

23. _____ is a method of running multiple independent virtual operating systems on a single physical hardware.
    A. Security topology
    B. Virtualization
    C. Cloud computing
    D. Risk management

24. Which of the following is defined as the method to create a virtual but dedicated connection between two ends?
    A. Virtualization
    B. Tunneling
    C. Encapsulation
    D. Symmetric algorithm

25. Infrastructure security deals with
    A. application of the risk management process
    B. how the protocol are used for providing network security
    C. how information flows and how work occurs in your network and systems
    D. physical security of the premises and hardware security

KEY (CORRECT ANSWERS)

1. A
2. C
3. C
4. A
5. B

6. A
7. D
8. B
9. B
10. A

11. B
12. D
13. D
14. D
15. A

16. A
17. D
18. C
19. B
20. A

21. C
22. D
23. B
24. B
25. C

EXAMINATION SECTION
TEST 1

DIRECTIONS: Each question or incomplete statement is followed by several suggested answers or completions. Select the one that BEST answers the question or completes the statement. *PRINT THE LETTER OF THE CORRECT ANSWER IN THE SPACE AT THE RIGHT.*

1. Which of the following protocols tends to be unsuitable for WAN VPN connections?
   A. PPP B. PPTP C. L2TP D. IPSec

2. To cope with the possibility of recovering sensitive data from computers which are donated or thrown away by companies, which of the following security policies is adopted by the companies?
   A. Acceptable use B. Disposal/destruction
   C. SLA D. Privacy

3. _____ tends to be defined as the combination of SSL and HTTP.
   A. TLS B. DES C. HTTPS D. PDQ

4. RAID _____ makes use of disk striping while using parity.
   A. 0 B. 1 C. 3 D. 5

5. While viewing activity logs, you suspect that an attack is underway. It appears as if TCP acknowledgements are being intercepted by a hacker causing the packets to be resent and subsequently intercepted by the hacker without the receiving computer's knowledge. What type of attack is this?
   A. Back door B. Rootkit
   C. Trojan horse D. Replay

6. Creating a policy which deals with how company information would be distributed and spreading the awareness among employees about the authorized personnel to deal with system and data information is effective for which type of attack?
   A. Mathematical B. DDoS
   C. Worm D. Social engineering

7. Which of the following tends to be a high-availability mechanism?
   A. RAID B. Switched networks
   C. Multiple CPU's D. Routing tables

8. Creating and implementing a disaster recovery plan (DRP) is mostly related to
   A. insurance coverage B. risk assessment
   C. media spin management D. ethical hacking

9. Which of the following does NOT fall under physical security control?
   A. Door locks
   B. Motion detectors
   C. Bulwark
   D. Strong passwords

10. Which of the following encryption processes makes use of one message to hide another?
    A. Steganography
    B. Hashing
    C. MDA
    D. Crypto-intelligence

11. Which of the following is NOT a viable security option for a user currently working on a confidential document who has been informed he must attend a meeting starting in two minutes?
    A. Log off
    B. Initiate the password-protected screen saver
    C. Immediately go to the meeting
    D. Shut down the system

12. Which type of attack uses a number of compromised hosts to focus on a single target?
    A. Hot site
    B. Phishing
    C. DDoS
    D. Targeted site

13. What technique or method can be employed by hackers and researchers to discover unknown flaws or errors in software?
    A. Dictionary attacks
    B. Fuzzing
    C. War dialing
    D. Cross-site request forgery

14. Which of the following is NOT a way to prevent or protect against XSS?
    A. Input validation
    B. Defensive coding
    C. Allowing script input
    D. Escaping meta-characters

15. Which of the following is another name for social engineering?
    A. Social disguise
    B. Social hacking
    C. Wetware
    D. Wetfire

16. The TCP/IP suite is broken into four architectural layers: Application layer, Internet layer, Network Access layer, and _____ layer.
    A. Host-to-Host or Transport
    B. Presentation
    C. Data
    D. OSI

17. _____ is used for Web Pages and World Wide.
    A. SMTP   B. TCP   C. HTTP   S. SSL

18. The default port for HTTPS is
    A. 443   B. 441   C. 442   D. 321

19. _____ is defined as the software or hardware tool used in order to determine, as well as block, unwanted interactions.
    A. Firewall
    B. URL filter
    C. Spam filter
    D. Protocol analyzer

20. The Spanning Tree Protocol (STP) operates at the _____ layer and makes sure there is only one active path between two stations.
    A. Application B. Presentation C. Network D. Data Link

21. Pretty Good Privacy is implemented for
    A. encryption
    B. e-mail security
    C. port security
    D. authorization

22. A firewall is used to apply protection against
    A. a virus
    B. a worm
    C. malware
    D. unauthenticated logins

23. When dealing with the tunnel mode using IPSec, it is used to protect the
    A. IP header only
    B. complete message
    C. complete IP packet
    D. IP protocol

24. A _____ cloud is a mixture of private and public cloud components.
    A. private B. public C. hybrid D. community

25. A _____ cloud is for internal use only.
    A. hybrid B. public C. secret D. private

KEY (CORRECT ANSWERS)

1.	A	11.	C
2.	B	12.	C
3.	C	13.	B
4.	D	14.	C
5.	D	15.	C
6.	D	16.	A
7.	A	17.	C
8.	B	18.	A
9.	D	19.	C
10.	A	20.	D

21.	B
22.	D
23.	C
24.	C
25.	D

TEST 2

DIRECTIONS: Each question or incomplete statement is followed by several suggested answers or completions. Select the one that BEST answers the question or completes the statement. *PRINT THE LETTER OF THE CORRECT ANSWER IN THE SPACE AT THE RIGHT.*

1. _____ is the basic element utilized to establish connectivity between the two nodes.
   A. Firewall
   B. Router
   C. Switch
   D. Protocol analyzer

2. _____ enables the groups of routers to share the routing information.
   A. Border Gateway Protocol (BGP)
   B. Routing Information Protocol (RIP)
   C. Open Shortest Path First (OSPF)
   D. Switch

3. Two types of routes are
   A. positive and negative
   B. 0 and 1
   C. static and dynamic
   D. configured and not configured

4. In Cisco, two main protocols are used, one being Gateway Routing Protocol (IGRP) and the other is
   A. TCP/IP
   B. SMTP
   C. UDP
   D. EIGRP

5. Which of the following is NOT an objective of a load balancer?
   A. Minimize cost
   B. Maximize throughput
   C. Reduce overloading
   D. Eliminate bottlenecks

6. Adware is the subset of
   A. malware
   B. spyware
   C. virus
   D. worms

7. _____ are able to launch many DoS as well as DDoS attacks which could be in any form like adware, spyware, and spam.
   A. Botnets
   B. Worms
   C. Viruses
   D. Trojans

8. _____ is defined as the type of malware which is intended to take control of a system to stop its usage and demanding payment for that.
   A. Malware
   B. Adware
   C. Ransomware
   D. Spyware

9. _____ is a type of malware which hides its identification and hence makes its elimination challenging.
   A. Armored virus
   B. Polymorphic malware
   C. Adware
   D. Trojans

10. _____ are defined as the kind of harmful code that intends to hid the recognition by means of signature.
    A. Polymorphic malware
    B. Armored virus
    C. Spyware
    D. Adware

11. The MOST vulnerable element when dealing with system security is
    A. information   B. people   C. software   D. hardware

12. The MOST crucial kind of loss that can be faced by an organization is of
    A. employee   B. data   C. software   D. hardware

13. _____ is defined as the recorded actions as performed by user over the internet.
    A. Virus   B. Worm   C. Cookie   D. Proxy

14. Antivirus is also called
    A. retrovirus
    B. armored virus
    C. macro virus
    D. vaccine

15. The secret keyword used to gain system access is known as
    A. IPSec
    B. password
    C. private key
    D. public key

16. Authentication is defined as
    A. verifying data integrity
    B. verifying user identity
    C. user authorization
    D. password protection

17. In cryptography, the output text is known as
    A. plain text
    B. block cipher
    C. cipher text
    D. encrypted text

18. Which of the following is NOT used for symmetric encryption?
    A. DES   B. SHA1   C. RC4   D. RSA

19. Protocol is defined as the
    A. rules and methods
    B. rules
    C. principles
    D. methods

20. The term cryptography is used to serve the purpose of
    A. testing
    B. development
    C. security
    D. analysis

21. The Media Access layer falls under the sub-layer of
    A. ANSI
    B. ASCII
    C. IEEE
    D. Data Link layer

22. SHF means
    A. Symmetric Hash Function
    B. Security Hashing Field
    C. System Hashing Function
    D. Symmetric Hashing Formation

23. Any loops which are created by flooding tends to be eliminated using
    A. RPF   B. SMTP   C. UDP   D. TCP

24. The routing table, which tends to be dynamic in nature, is updated 24.____
    A. instantly   B. manually   C. periodically   D. randomly

25. When dealing with IPV4, the packets which are transferred are known as 25.____
    A. spoofing   B. datagram
    C. data packets   D. data segments

KEY (CORRECT ANSWERS)

1.	B		11.	B
2.	A		12.	B
3.	C		13.	C
4.	D		14.	D
5.	A		15.	B
6.	B		16.	B
7.	A		17.	C
8.	C		18.	D
9.	A		19.	A
10.	A		20.	C

21. C
22. B
23. A
24. C
25. B

TEST 3

DIRECTIONS: Each question or incomplete statement is followed by several suggested answers or completions. Select the one that BEST answers the question or completes the statement. *PRINT THE LETTER OF THE CORRECT ANSWER IN THE SPACE AT THE RIGHT.*

1. Round Robin is one of the techniques of
   A. Routing
   B. Load Balancing
   C. Encryption
   D. Network Security

   1.____

2. *Destination to every packet is assigned randomly.* This definition refers to which of the following techniques?
   A. Round Robin
   B. Random Choice
   C. Preferences
   D. Load Monitoring

   2.____

3. Which of the following is NOT an additional function performed by Load Balancing?
   A. Caching
   B. Secure Sockets Layer (SSL) offloading
   C. Data encapsulation
   D. Buffering

   3.____

4. NAT is defined as
   A. Network Address Translation
   B. Network Access Translation
   C. Network Access Transference
   D. Non Accessible Translation

   4.____

5. A _____ is defined as the interaction tunnel between two nodes while using an intermediate network.
   A. switch
   B. router
   C. firewall
   D. Virtual Private Network (VPN)

   5.____

6. _____ is the type of virus which transforms and changes other programs as well as databases.
   A. Stealth   B. Phage   C. Companion   D. Retrovirus

   6.____

7. Those viruses which prevent their identification by masking themselves from applications are known as
   A. stealth   B. phage   C. companion   D. retrovirus

   7.____

8. Which of the following are able to side step the antivirus software?
   A. Stealth   B. Phage   C. Companion   D. Retrovirus

   8.____

9. The viruses which use update/software patches intended to upgrade software programs are known as
   A. macro viruses   B. stealth   C. phage   D. companion

   9.____

10. _____ spoofing is NOT a type of spoofing attack.
    A. IP   B. TCP   C. ARP   D. DNS

11. When dealing with asymmetric key cryptography, _____ keeps the private key.
    A. sender
    B. both sender and receiver
    C. receiver
    D. all connected to the internet

12. DES is known as Data
    A. Encryption Software
    B. Encryption Solution
    C. Encapsulation Standard
    D. Encryption Standard

13. DES deals with _____ cipher.
    A. block   B. brick   C. bit   D. packet

14. Cryptanalysis is defined as the process of
    A. data encryption
    B. data encapsulation
    C. data migration
    D. diagnosing insecurity within the cryptographic process

15. In order to interact with the SSH server, which of the following TCP ports is used?
    A. 21   B. 32   C. 22   D. 41

16. Decryption of the encrypted message takes place at the
    A. sender
    B. receiver
    C. sender and receiver
    D. intruder

17. The term DSS means Digital
    A. Standard for Security
    B. System of Standards
    C. Signature System
    D. Signature Standard

18. The term *One Way Authentication* is referred to as
    A. no transfer
    B. double transfer
    C. half duplex transfer
    D. single transfer of information

19. The term *Two Way Authentication* is referred to as
    A. no transfer
    B. double transfer
    C. half duplex transfer
    D. single transfer of information

20. DHCP tends to be used in order to provide _____ to the Host.
    A. URL   B. HTTP   C. IP   D. Proxy

21. IP was initially proposed to sever the purpose of
    A. tunneling
    B. scheduling
    C. unicast delivery
    D. multicast delivery

22. Tunneling is defined as the process used on the two systems that are operating
    A. IPV6   B. IPV2   C. IPV4   D. IPSec

23. Substitution Cipher replaces one symbol with
    A. other
    B. two symbols
    C. three symbols
    D. keys

24. The proxy firewall performs its actions at the _____ layer.
    A. Application   B. Datalink   C. Support   D. Presentation

25. The division of data into block as done by SSL is
    A. 2*3   B. 2*10   C. 2*14   D. 2*20

KEY (CORRECT ANSWERS)

1.	B	11.	C
2.	C	12.	D
3.	C	13.	A
4.	A	14.	D
5.	D	15.	C
6.	B	16.	B
7.	A	17.	D
8.	D	18.	D
9.	A	19.	C
10.	B	20.	C

21.	C
22.	A
23.	A
24.	A
25.	C

TEST 4

DIRECTIONS: Each question or incomplete statement is followed by several suggested answers or completions. Select the one that BEST answers the question or completes the statement. *PRINT THE LETTER OF THE CORRECT ANSWER IN THE SPACE AT THE RIGHT.*

1. Which of the following is NOT the name of VPN Concentrator? 1.____
   A. VPN Server
   B. VPN Provider
   C. VPN Gateway
   D. VPN Firewall

2. Which of the following is NOT an example of Rule Based Management Tool? 2.____
   A. Firewalls   B. Proxies   C. Routers   D. Switch

3. _____ tends to reduce the probability of DoS attacks. 3.____
   A. Data Encapsulation
   B. Encryption
   C. Flood Guard
   D. Load Balancing

4. _____ tends to act as a proxy among the local area network and the internet. 4.____
   A. NAT   B. VPN   C. IPSec   D. Router

5. Which of the following is NOT the area in which virtualization can be implemented? 5.____
   A. Server
   B. Application
   C. Presentation
   D. Network

6. _____ deals with the actual danger under consideration. 6.____
   A. Risk   B. Threat   C. Vulnerability   D. Virus

7. _____ deals with likely causes associated with the risk. 7.____
   A. Risk   B. Threat   C. Vulnerability   D. Virus

8. _____ deals with where the system is weak. 8.____
   A. Risk   B. Threat   C. Vulnerability   D. Virus

9. Which of the following is an attack in which a hacker configures his or her system as a twin of the legitimate wireless access point? 9.____
   A. Evil Twin
   B. War Diving
   C. Bluejacking
   D. Packet Sniffing

10. Which of the following is regarded as spam over IM? 10.____
    A. IP spoofing
    B. DNS spoofing
    C. Spim
    D. Phishing

11. SSH-2 lacks which of the following layers? 11.____
    A. Transport
    B. Physical
    C. Connection
    D. User Authentication

12. SCP is the protocol which is based on which of the following over SSH?
    A. SMTP B. TCP C. RCP D. DHCP

13. Which of the following TCP ports is used by SMTP?
    A. 25 B. 35 C. 45 D. 55

14. SMTP is used for message
    A. transport B. encryption C. content D. delivery

15. FTP makes use of how many TCP connections that are running in parallel for file transfer?
    A. 2 B. 4 C. 6 D. 8

16. DHCP tends to make use of port _____ for sending information.
    A. 62 B. 63 C. 65 D. 67

17. While communicating on the same subnet, DHCP client and server use
    A. UDP Broadcast B. TCP Broadcast
    C. SMTP D. FTP

18. When the IP address is achieved, which of the following is used in order to be able to avoid IP conflict?
    A. Address resolution protocol B. IP conflict resolution
    C. Changing the IP address D. Gateway protocol

19. The protocol ICMP tends to be utilized for
    A. Ifconfig B. Traceroute
    C. Ping D. Ping and Traceroute

20. The process of signing the message while sending is known as
    A. Digital System B. Digital Signature
    C. Digital Text D. Encryption

21. When working with an asymmetric key, _____ key is used.
    A. 2 B. 3 C. 4 D. 5

22. SNMP exists in _____ versions.
    A. 3 B. 4 C. 5 D. 2

23. SNMPv3 has improved _____ compared to SNMPv2.
    A. speed B. precision C. security D. accuracy

24. The SHA-1 consists of a message comprising _____ bits.
    A. 1000 B. 512 C. 820 D. 160

25. _____ Cipher is referred to as the Transposition Cipher.
    A. Block b. Playfair C. Caesar D. Multi

KEY (CORRECT ANSWERS)

1.	B	11.	B
2.	D	12.	C
3.	C	13.	A
4.	A	14.	A
5.	D	15.	A
6.	A	16.	D
7.	B	17.	A
8.	C	18.	A
9.	A	19.	D
10.	C	20.	B

21. A
22. D
23. C
24. D
25. B

www.ingramcontent.com/pod-product-compliance
Lightning Source LLC
Chambersburg PA
CBHW082046300426
44117CB00015B/2629